Sea Turtles
of the world

Text and photography by
Doug Perrine

Voyageur Press

Acknowledgments

So many persons and organizations have assisted with my photography and research for this book that it would be impossible to name them all. I would like, however, to mention a few that have been particularly helpful. I hope those who have been inadvertently omitted will forgive the oversight.

Photography of Critically Endangered Kemp's ridley sea turtles nesting at Rancho Nuevo, Mexico, was made possible through the generous assistance of the National Save the Sea Turtle Foundation, and with the permission of the Instituto Nacional de la Pesca (I.N.P.) and Centro Regional de Investigación Pesquera (C.R.I.P.) of the Mexican government, and the Gladys Porter Zoo.

Special thanks are also due to my scientific advisers who reviewed the manuscript and made numerous helpful suggestions, George Balazs and Nicolas Pilcher. Responsibility for any errors and misinterpretations, however, is mine. Additional thanks to Wayne Witzell, who supplied numerous helpful documents and advice, to Kris Anderson, librarian extraordinaire, without whose expert assistance this book could have never been completed, and to (in no particular order), Jean-Michel Cousteau, Dick and Phyllis Dresie, Jannie Bech Sperling,

Randall Arauz, Larry Wood, Rene Marquez, Pat Burchfield, Jaime Pena, Peter Barrett, Martin Sanchez, Alejandro Arenas, Paul Basintal, Sabah Parks, Azimah Jumatli, Jen Homcy, Stacy Van Santen, Wayne Pedroso, Borneo Divers, Laura Sarti, Scott Eckert, Karen Eckert, John Hewitt, Tom Schmidt, Richie Moretti, Sue Schaff, Pamela Plotkin, Brendan Godley & Annette Broderick, Catherine Bell, Peter Lutz, Molly Lutcavage, Karen Bjorndal, Lisa Diaz, Jim Watt, Rene Umberger, Peter Bennett & Ursula Keuper-Bennett, Gene Gaffney, David Bull, Bruce Koike, Ken Hydes, Frank Wojcik, Gustavo Hernandez, Hector Martinez, Norma Cruz, Ethel Arias, Javier & Maria Martinez, Harun Rahman, Jeff Ripple, Ron Orenstein, Howard Hall, Jim Robinson, Colin Limpus, Jeff Schmid, Jon Houghton, Laura Sarti, George Zug, Jeffrey Polovina, Sallie Beavers, Mike McCoy, John Parmenter, Robert Pitman, Michael Frick, Kendra and Dayna Coufal, Todd Steiner, Frank Wojcik, and Marc Rice.

I also owe a debt of gratitude to the late Archie Carr, the "father" of sea turtle research and conservation, who inspired us all, and to all of his "children," the researchers who followed in his footsteps, and from whose published works the information in this book is drawn.

Text copyright © 2003 by Doug Perrine
Photographs copyright © 2003 by Doug Perrine, except where noted for individual photographs

Edited by Kari Cornell
Designed by JoDee Mittlestadt
Printed in China

03 04 05 06 07   5 4 3 2 1

Library of Congress Cataloging-in-Publication Data

Perrine, Doug.
  Sea turtles of the world / text and photography by Doug Perrine.
      p. cm.—(WorldLife discovery guides)
  Includes bibliographical references (p.140).
  ISBN 0-89658-555-7 (hardcover)
  1. Sea turtles. I. Title. II. Series.
  QL666.C536 P42 2003
  597.92'8—dc21

                    2002154118

Distributed in Canada by Raincoast Books
9050 Shaughnessy Street, Vancouver, B.C. V6P 6E5

Published by Voyageur Press, Inc.
123 North Second Street, P.O. Box 338
Stillwater, MN 55082 U.S.A.
651-430-2210, fax 651-430-2211
books@voyageurpress.com
www.voyageurpress.com

Educators, fundraisers, premium and gift buyers, publicists, and marketing managers: Looking for creative products and new sales ideas? Voyageur Press books are available at special discounts when purchased in quantities, and special editions can be created to your specifications. For details contact the marketing department at 800-888-9653.

Frontispiece: green turtle

Full title: Kemp's ridley sea turtle

Title inset : leatherback hatchling

Contents: loggerhead turtle, Bahamas

Contents

Foreword

by Jean-Michel Cousteau

While diving the coral reef, you'll experience few things as exciting as soaring weightless over what appears to be a feature of the ocean floor, then having it blink, move, and slowly take flight. This is the joy of finding and following the sea turtle—its movement is majestic, often slow—and like so many experiences under water, it evokes its own music, its own tone. In the case of sea turtles, the music is that of a bass fiddle with deep, slow tones capable of great range, the sound of dignity itself.

In this book, Doug Perrine's text and photos strike exactly the right chord of what we need to know about sea turtles in a style that makes good science conversational. From my perspective of over fifty years diving, exploring and advocating for the ocean, I especially appreciate the emphasis Doug places on the fate of the sea turtle as linked to human population and behavior. I go a step further and believe that if we protect the ocean, we protect ourselves, and that almost any sea creature can serve as an example of what has gone wrong and what must now happen if things are to get better. There is cause for hope, but there is also a serious deadline or we will lose more than we could ever mourn, and nothing will be the same. The timeline of life has a rift we must repair.

The timeline of Perrine's investigation of the sea turtle is the long view, from the world in which sea turtles evolved, to a contemporary species-by-species description and status and, in some cases, current attempts to save them. Sea turtles evolved in an ancient world of extremes, have survived two mass extinctions, and now face an unprecedented third, mostly induced by our own species.

The tremendous value of this book you now hold is that it presents us with a wondrous view of what we may lose or, more optimistically, what we may be inspired to save. Perrine documents that, within a blink of time, we are learning amazing things about creatures we have recognized only for their use to us. The turtle that much of the world sees as an ingredient in soups is capable of some of the most amazing feats and is, of itself and apart from us, astounding.

You cannot read this book and absorb the information Perrine presents and ever think of the sea turtle in the same way. The facts are fascinating, but put together, the story of this animal's life seems alien and excites the imagination.

For example: Some species of sea turtles may not reach sexual maturity until age sixty! Given that females return to the beaches where they were hatched, this means that they hold the memory of their nesting beach for all those years, then swim thousands of miles of open ocean, and find the beach perfectly the first time, using an ability to navigate that baffles scientists.

Perrine offers several theories for how sea turtles navigate and describes one that is a startlingly fresh perspective of the ocean world: Once close to their native beach, some species of sea turtles may be guided by the signature sound of how the surf breaks on their stretch of coast. The subtle combination of factors at a habitat creates its own unique tone, its own melody that means everything to these turtles. They are guided home by the song of the sea in one of nature's more elegant cycles.

It is particularly satisfying to me that they may recognize that particular beach by its sound, one of the many notes of the ocean's complex symphony, of nature's magnificent aria for life. Each animal and species and habitat contributes to the sound of our planet. Each note counts. With each disappearance, the song becomes more silent. With each recovery, there is more melody, more complex harmonies, and the orchestration of the sea is enriched. The turtle must play its part. So must we.

Kemp's ridley sea turtle hatchlings struggle to the sea after release from a protected nesting area. In the sea, as on land, their survival will depend largely upon the actions of humans.

Foreword

By Karen A. Bjorndal

Archie Carr Center for Sea Turtle Research and Deparment of Zoology, University of Florida

Sea Turtles of the World is a splendid book that captures the beauty of sea turtles underwater. Those people fortunate enough to have viewed sea turtles in the wild have usually seen either females lumbering up a beach to deposit their eggs or hatchlings scurrying frantically on the return trip from their nest to the sea. Although both scenes are impressive and leave lasting impressions, one does not gain an appreciation of the grace and beauty of sea turtles. On land, sea turtles are out of their element, and their movements are laborious and clumsy. Sea turtles are designed for life in the oceans—to appreciate their grace and agility, sea turtles must be viewed underwater as they fly past on their flipper wings.

Our understanding of the biology of sea turtles has improved substantially over recent years. Few studies, however, have evaluated the roles of sea turtles in marine ecosystems. Just as much of the beauty of sea turtles is lost when they are viewed only on land, much of the fascination and importance of sea turtles is lost when they are only considered as isolated species rather than as integral parts of marine ecosystems.

Populations of sea turtles have been drastically reduced since interactions between humans and sea turtles began. Before sea turtle populations were depleted by humans, sea turtles occurred in massive numbers that are now difficult to imagine. These population declines have produced a corresponding decline in the extent to which sea turtles fulfill their roles in maintaining the structure and function of marine ecosystems. At high population levels, sea turtles played major roles in marine systems as consumers, prey, and competitors; as hosts for parasites and pathogens; as substrates for epibionts; as nutrient transporters; and as modifiers of the landscape.

In their roles as consumers, sea turtles prey upon a large number and diverse array of prey species. Worldwide, loggerheads feed upon well over 200 species; at least ninety-four species are consumed by loggerheads in shallow water habitats in eastern Australia alone. In the Caribbean, hawksbills feed primarily on sponges in reef habitats. Corals and sponges compete for space on reefs, and sponges are more often the superior competitor. Before the massive decline in hawksbills as a result of the tortoiseshell trade, hawksbills, by consuming sponges, influenced space competition and thus affected the structure and diversity of Caribbean reefs. Green turtles, the only herbivorous sea turtle, had perhaps an even more dramatic effect on seagrass ecosystems. The green turtle population in the Caribbean today is estimated to represent only 3 to 7 percent of pre-exploitation population levels. At natural population densities, green turtles grazed seagrass pastures extensively. Grazed seagrass pastures with blade lengths of 2 to 4 cm would have very different patterns of biodiversity, productivity, and structure than the essentially ungrazed pastures of today with blade lengths of up to 30 cm or more. In grazed seagrass pastures, nutrient cycling times are significantly shortened, time for epibiont colonization of seagrass blades is reduced, and shorter seagrass blades decrease the entrapment of particles and deposition of substrate. Thus, the physical structure of seagrass ecosystems that are important nursery areas for many species of fish and invertebrates have been substantially changed with the decline of green turtles.

Sea turtles also play an important role as prey and, particularly at small sizes, are consumed by a wide range of predators. Risk of predation is assumed to be greatest at early life stages and to decline as sea turtles attain larger sizes and thus outgrow many of their predators. Sea turtle eggs and hatchlings are important food resources for many predators, including crabs, ants, raccoons, coatis, foxes, birds, and fish. Large sea turtles, however, are not free of predation. In the water, major predators are crocodiles, killer whales, and sharks, particularly tiger sharks and, in the Mediterranean, white sharks. While on the nesting beach, adult females may fall prey to jaguars and pumas.

Sea turtles can take on the appearance of underwater gardens. A vast array of marine organisms, including barnacles, amphipods and algae, attach to the shell and skin of sea turtles, using the turtles as a mobile substrate. Loggerheads apparently support the largest and most diverse set of epibionts. Loggerheads nesting in the southeastern United States host 100 species from thirteen phyla, and loggerheads nesting at Xcacel, Mexico, carry thirty-seven species of algae with up to twelve species on an individual turtle. The ramifications of these epibiont loads for the turtles are not clear. Sea turtles may benefit from being camouflaged by their epibionts, but the drag resulting from epibionts increases the energetic costs of swimming. Of course, life is not always easy for the epibionts. They may be killed when sea turtles scrape against hard objects or bury themselves in mud; epibionts that cannot withstand desiccation may die when female sea turtles emerge on land to nest.

Perhaps most fascinating are the roles of sea turtles in modifying their habitats. The reproductive migrations of female sea turtles transport large quantities of nutrients from nutrient-rich foraging grounds to nutrient-poor nesting beaches. Because sea turtles usually do not feed to any great extent during their sojourn at the nesting beach, the energy and nutrients contained in the eggs deposited on the nesting beach are derived from the distant foraging grounds. On Florida nesting beaches, less than a third of the energy and nitrogen deposited in the loggerhead eggs are returned to the ocean in the form of hatchlings. Substantial proportions of nutrients enter the terrestrial ecosystem and some are absorbed by dune vegetation. By providing nutrients to dune vegetation, loggerheads may help stabilize the nesting environment upon which they depend for successful reproduction.

Green turtles are also known to maintain the quality of their nesting beach on Heron Island, Australia, by holding the nesting beach habitat in arrested succession. Green turtles prevent the spread of inland forests onto the beach by uprooting seedlings while nesting. These activities maintain an open habitat essential for successful reproduction.

Sea turtles also modify underwater habitats. Infaunal mining—a foraging behavior in which loggerheads excavate trenches by sweeping soft substrate aside with their front flippers to expose infaunal prey—may have substantial effects on substrate characteris-

A green turtle passes a school of bigeye jacks on the reef surrounding Sipadan Island in Sabah, Malaysia. Both the jacks and the turtle are in "rest mode." The jacks feed at night, while the turtle feeds on seagrasses that are not found on the reef.

tics such as compaction, aeration, and nutrient distribution. Hawaiian green turtles transform coral heads to coral rubble during foraging activities and while using coral heads as "scratching posts."

I have highlighted only some of the roles of sea turtles in their ecosystems. Few have been studied, and many more await discovery. While these studies continue, take the opportunity to enter the fascinating world of sea turtles and marvel at their beauty in *Sea Turtles of the World*.

Author's Preface

In the 1950s, the late, revered Dr. Archie Carr Jr. was perhaps the only scientist in the world who specialized in the study of the natural history of sea turtles. Today hundreds of dedicated scientists publish their research findings, revising our understanding of sea turtle biology on a constant basis. Since I first began photographing and reading about sea turtles in the 1980s, our view of these extraordinary animals has changed dramatically.

For example, green turtles, once thought of as simple reptiles, are now known to have a fascinating and complex life history. So complex, in fact, that if translated into terrestrial terms, the life cycle of a green turtle would include several forms. As a land-dweller, the sea turtle might be born as an earthworm in Florida. After burrowing out of the ground, the earthworm would spend the next decade as a bird, flying around the continent feeding on insects. The bird would then drop to earth to live out the next twenty-five years as a cow, grazing in Oregon pastures. Finally, the cow would march back to Florida, where it originally hatched, to bury some earthworm eggs.

Some discoveries have affected sea turtle conservation efforts, making them much more difficult. At one time, for instance, researchers believed that sea turtles took six years to reproduce. Ridley turtles, and perhaps leatherbacks, do mature in ten years or less. But other sea turtles often take twenty to thirty years to mature and reproduce. Age at sexual maturity is one of the key defining characteristics that control the population dynamics of any species.

The time required to reach sexual maturity is but one of several critical parameters of biology and life history that vary among the seven species of sea turtles. Each species has unique habits and characteristics. In addition to important differences among species, recent research has revealed that there can be surprising biological differences among various populations of the same species of sea turtle, and among individuals within a population. Therefore, it is important to keep in mind that the extreme ends of a range of values for a biological parameter may not be at all typical of the majority of animals within a population or species. At the same time, what is average for a species may not be representative of all populations, let alone all individuals. Such large variation can be confusing, but it is good—it is the raw material of evolution.

When writing this book, I found it necessary to use a number of technical terms, so I have included a glossary and a diagram of basic sea turtle anatomy for your reference. Scientists sometimes disagree over the usage and spelling of both common and scientific names and terms. I have attempted to use the form most commonly accepted at the time of this writing, for example *kempi* and *agassizi*, rather than *kempii* and *agassizii*, and sea turtle, rather than seaturtle. I have used some forms, such as green turtle and green sea turtle, interchangeably.

Disagreements over biological and conservation status can be very passionate. Is the black sea turtle a species, *Chelonia agassizi,* or is it a subspecies—the eastern Pacific green turtle, *Chelonia mydas agassizi*? Researchers are divided, but at the time of publication, a majority seemed to favor subspecies status, so that is how I have classified it in the book. Bear in mind that this opinion could shift with future discoveries. New research methods may determine that what appears to be a single species is actually a complex of two or more species or vice-versa. This is the nature of biology—answers are not presented on stone tablets, but rather formulated from the best available information at any given time. This book is, therefore, a snapshot of what we believe to be true about sea turtles at the time of publication.

Posthatchling green turtles crowd a tank at the Cayman Turtle Farm. They are rarely seen in the wild at this stage of their complex life cycle.

A First Glimpse

ABOVE: *A mature male olive ridley sea turtle, accompanied by pilot fish, cruises offshore from a nesting beach in Costa Rica.*

LEFT: *This beach, which appears to be strewn with boulders, is actually covered with a "fleet" of female olive ridleys, coming ashore to lay their eggs. The males wait offshore, hoping to mate with females that have not yet had their eggs fertilized.*

Standing alone on a remote beach on the Pacific coast of Costa Rica, I gaped in awe as wave after wave of armored, prehistoric-looking beasts emerged from the water and crawled up onto the shore, leaving tractor-like patterns across the entire beach. Sea turtles (olive ridleys in this case) are modern animals, but they are so similar in appearance to their ancestors, which shared the earth with dinosaurs, that it was easy to imagine that I was back in the Age of Reptiles. Yet here I stood on a beach in the year 2000, witnessing a mass nesting or "arribada" of nearly half a million sea turtles—creatures that had been decimated in nearby areas by industrial harvesting only two decades earlier. This arribada was convincing evidence that rational management can allow some populations of threatened creatures to recover from the disastrous effects of human settlement and activity. Most of the news about sea turtles and other endangered species is bad, but the return of some immense olive ridley arribadas is a tangible beacon of hope, and a clear indication that the future of this and many other species lies almost entirely in our hands.

Already, hundreds of turtles crowded the beach. Thousands more swam just beyond the breakers, waiting for their turn to come ashore and lay their eggs. I kicked off my shoes and waded into the foam, hoping to catch a picture of a turtle emerging from a wave onto the beach. I felt a sharp pain in my leg and looked down to see blood beginning to seep out of a fresh gash just above my ankle. The turtle that had sliced me open with the edge of her shell as she surfed into shore was trundling up the beach, intent on her reproductive mission. "Great," I thought. "Now I can add ninja surfer turtles to the long list of hazards facing the professional marine life photographer!"

The turtles plowing up the beach were not only

ABOVE: Olive ridley arribadas, or mass emergences of females coming ashore to nest, typically start at night but continue into daylight hours, often lasting for several days.

FACING PAGE: In the 1980s, Norine Rouse of Palm Beach, Florida, (known as the "Turtle Lady") demonstrated that loggerhead turtles often return to the same undersea ledges each year, and can recognize and respond to humans who treat them with respect and consideration.

This immature hawksbill foraging in Grand Cayman waters probably hatched in either Cuba (75 percent chance) or Mexico (20 percent chance). Both of these countries protect turtles within their own waters, but in the Cayman Islands, licensed fishermen may legally capture the turtles.

oblivious to me, but to other turtles as well. They crawled over one another as if the nesting turtles were rocks or logs. Under such crowded nesting conditions, a female turtle digging in the sand to bury her eggs will often unearth eggs laid by other turtles. Due in large part to such nest destruction and the bacterial and fungal contamination that results, hatching success is much lower on this beach than on others where turtles nest individually. Driven by instinct, sea turtles continue to nest in places where they may have very little chance of producing offspring, and will even continue to lay their eggs as a predatory animal eats them, or as a human takes them. This limited ability to adapt to changing circumstances is one of the great obstacles facing sea turtles as they struggle to survive in a rapidly changing world.

Turtles and Humans

More than 200 million years after the first turtle appeared on the earth (compared with half a million years for humans), and after surviving one or more great catastrophes that wiped out most life on the planet, sea turtles face a very precarious future. A number of changes in the earth's environment, most of which are related in some way to rapid human population growth, threaten the sea turtle's livelihood. A series of extinctions has already begun that threatens to sweep away much of the planet's diversity. Without a change in the human population trend, turtles and many other wild animals face a very bleak future.

Sea turtles' ability (or inability) to adapt to environmental changes may play an important role in their survival (or extinction). At times sea turtles show a surprising ability to alter their habits. When large-scale harvesting of sea turtles began in the Hawaiian Islands, for example, green sea turtles switched to feeding at night. Eventually, after years of protection under the Endangered Species Act, they once again started to swim into shallow areas to feed by day. They have now become so tolerant of humans that they will feed right among the legs of wading tourists. The fact that sea turtles have begun to nest on newly created artificial beaches shows that even a rigidly fixed behavior such as the choice of nesting beaches can be modified in some individuals. Recent experiments show that turtles are more capable of learning than had previously been believed. Turtles can adapt their behavior to take advantage of newly available food sources. However, such changes often take place over long periods of time. A sea turtle cannot quickly analyze a situation and solve an immediate problem. Videos of sea turtles caught in the path of an approaching trawl net, for example, reveal that rather than ducking out of the net's path, the turtle will continue to swim ahead until it is so exhausted that it falls back into the net.

Unfortunately, our world is changing so fast that sea turtles could never adapt quickly enough to save themselves. Human decisions alone will determine the fate of sea turtles. In many cases, we have risen to this challenge and modified our own behavior in order to give sea turtles a chance to live. The harvest of sea turtles is prohibited in most countries, and technological innovations, such as TEDs (which allow turtles to escape from trawl nets) have decreased unintentional mortality. Protection of nesting beaches and imposed measures to reduce capture in fisheries have brought the Kemp's ridley sea turtle back from the brink of extinction.

But the new threats sea turtles face will not be easy to counteract. Many biologists believe that the long-term survival of these animals is no longer threatened so much by direct harvesting as by large-scale environmental changes. In many areas, sea turtles are no longer hunted, but are still dying due to illnesses that could be related to pollution and global warming. Many turtles are killed by fishing gear that is not intended for turtles, but has become so ubiquitous in their environment that they cannot avoid it. Although in many areas people are no longer harvesting turtles or their eggs from nesting beaches, turtle reproduction remains threatened due to development, erosion, light pollution, and other changes that make the beaches no longer suitable for hatching baby turtles. Some of these problems can be addressed with easy fixes, such as shielding beachfront lighting, but most are complex dilemmas without easy solutions.

Perhaps the most important step humans can take

Mexican schoolchildren are introduced to a national treasure—hatchling Kemp's ridley sea turtles, which breed only in their country. Educational programs like this one at Rancho Nuevo are critical to ensuring that future generations will care for the earth's natural resources responsibly rather than squander them, as has too often occurred in the past.

toward sea turtle preservation is to control our own population. But such a dramatic change will not come easily. Human attitudes toward reproduction are based in deeply rooted instincts and cultural and religious traditions that are highly resistant to change. In the end it will be our own flexibility, rather than that of turtles, which seals their fate. It is my fervent hope that every reader of this book will have no more than four grandchildren, every one of whom will have the opportunity to see a great armada of armored reptiles emerge from the ocean to fling sand wildly about on some remote, untamed beach.

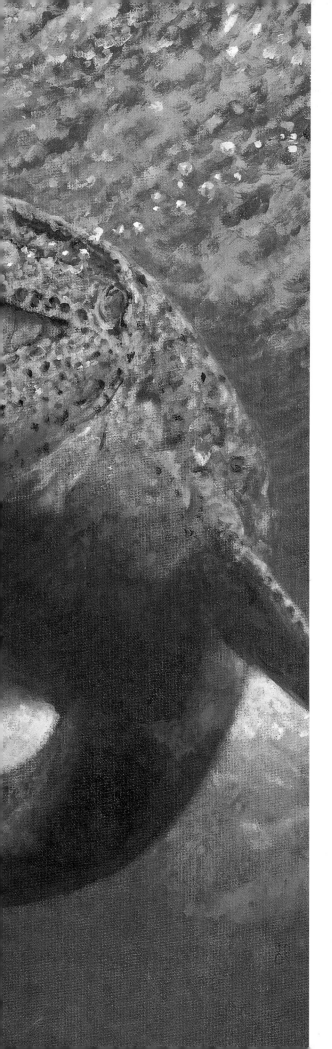

CHAPTER 1

Origins and Ancestors

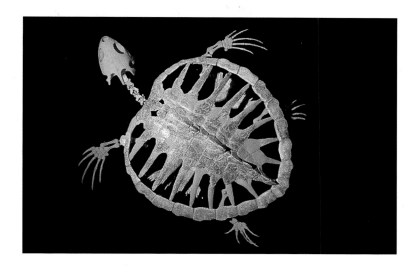

ABOVE: A fossil Toxochelys *from about 75 million years ago shows the lightweight shell design common in its family, which died out about 40 million years ago. When this turtle was alive, the openings in the carapace would have been covered with skin or horny plates. This specimen is on display at the Smithsonian Natural History Museum.*

LEFT: The remarkable spikes on the carapace of Calcarichelys, *known as the "thorny protostegid" from the late Cretaceous period (more than 65 million years ago), did not prevent a mosasaur (a prehistoric swimming reptile) from occasionally consuming one as a meal. At about about 12 feet (4 m), the* Clidastes *in this photograph was one of the smallest mosasaurs of the time, making it food for larger mosasaurs. Illustration © Dan Varner.*

The evolutionary origin of turtles has been called "one of the great unanswered questions of evolutionary biology." The scientific community does not know from what group of primitive reptiles turtles descended. The oldest known turtle fossils, discovered in Germany, Greenland, and Thailand (countries once part of the supercontinent Pangea), belong to the extinct genus *Proganochelys* and are believed to be about 210 million years old. *Proganochelys* looked very much like modern turtles, but possessed something that none of today's turtles have—tiny teeth, located on the roof of the mouth. It also had spikes on its neck and tail. *Proganochelys* may have been either terrestrial or an amphibious swamp-dweller. The fact that all turtles lay their eggs on land is a strong clue that the first turtle was a terrestrial animal. Evidence

Proganochelys, the earliest known turtle, is believed to be an evolutionary dead-end, and not an ancestor of modern turtles. Both Proganochelys *and today's turtles must be descended from earlier ancestors whose fossilized remains have not yet been found. Illustration © David W. Miller / Seapics.com.*

indicates, however, that the first turtles must have evolved even earlier than 210 million years ago.

A little more than 200 million years ago, at the beginning of the Jurassic period, a mass extinction occurred, the second in the earth's history. Both dinosaurs and turtles survived and thrived. Turtles flourished throughout the Age of Reptiles, or Mesozoic era (245 to 65 million years ago), producing many more species and families than there are today, including such bizarre forms as the horned turtles, or meiolaniids. These had goat-like or steer-like horns, giving the skulls the appearance of devil masks. The majority of these families were aquatic, living in both freshwater and marine habitats. The adaptation to living in the sea occurred not once, but a number of times in different groups of turtles, so the transition from life in a coastal marsh to swimming in the ocean must not have been too difficult.

Scientists speculate that about the time turtles had achieved their greatest diversity (approximately 65 million years ago), a giant asteroid may have collided with the earth, causing the next mass extinction. Dinosaurs were wiped out, except for the group that evolved into birds, but some turtles survived and continued to evolve.

Sea Turtle Beginnings

The oldest marine turtle fossils found date from the Jurassic period (208 to 145 million years ago). By that time, the main lineage of turtles had split into two branches: the side-neck turtles (pleurodires), which protect the head by folding the neck and head over to one side, and the hidden-neck or arch-neck turtles (cryptodires), which pull the neck into a vertical S-curve and retract the head straight back between the shoulders. The side-necked turtles produced many seagoing species during the Cretaceous period (145 to 65 million years ago), but all of these died out. Modern pleurodires live in freshwater. Jurassic sea turtles belonged to the hidden-neck group, the group to which more turtles belong today. Many families once made up the hidden-neck group, but most died out by the early part of the Cretaceous period.

Four important families of hidden-neck sea turtles did survive into the mid-Cretaceous period. Two of these families, the Dermochelyidae and the Cheloniidae, have modern descendants. The leatherback sea turtle is the only surviving member of the Dermochelyidae. All other modern sea turtles belong to the Cheloniidae.

Archelon, *the largest sea turtle that ever lived, could reach a length of 15 feet (4.5 m) with a head 3.3 feet (1 m) long and a span of 16.5 feet (5.25 m) between the tips of its flippers. This Archelon lived about 75 million years ago and may have weighed two to five tons. Photo © Ed Gerken / Black Hills Inst., Hill City, SD.*

The leatherback family (Dermochelyidae) may be related to the extinct family Protostegidae, which included not only the giants Protostega *and* Archelon, *but also the diminutive* Santanachelys, *which measured a mere 8 inches (20 cm).*

Extinct Species

The extinct Toxochelyidae appear to be related to the Cheloniidae. They were small- to medium-sized, round-shelled sea turtles. Some had upper shells of solid bone like modern sea turtles, while other members of the family had much lighter upper shells with large openings, most likely an adaptation for open ocean existence. In life these openings would have been covered with skin or horny plates. *Toxochelys*, the best-known member of this family, had eye sockets that faced up, suggesting that the turtle may have been a bottom-dweller. The toxochelyids died out by the late Eocene (56 to 37 million years ago).

The extinct Protostegidae may be related to the Dermochelyidae. Like the toxochelyids, many of the protestegids had frame-type shells with gaps between the bones, and probably lived in open ocean. Although most later protostegids were large to gigantic sea turtles with huge heads, the earliest known protostegid, *Santanachelys*, from 110 million years ago, was only 8 inches (20 cm) long. Like modern fresh-water turtles, *Santanachelys* had highly flexible flippers with movable digits, but, like marine-dwelling turtles, it also had large salt-excreting glands, indicating that it lived in the ocean. Later protostegids had semi-rigid flippers like modern sea turtles. This family includes the giants *Protostega* and *Archelon*, the latter being the largest sea turtle that ever lived.

Archelon inhabited the Western Interior Seaway, or Niobrara Sea, which covered the middle of the North American continent, separating the Rocky Mountains from the eastern half of the continent, and connecting the Arctic Ocean to the Gulf of Mexico. One *Archelon* fossil is 15 feet (4.5 m) long from beak to tail, with a span of 16.5 feet (5.25 m) between the extended tips of its massive flippers. Estimates of the creature's weight range from 4,500 to 11,000 pounds (2–5 metric tons). *Archelon*'s huge head alone could be

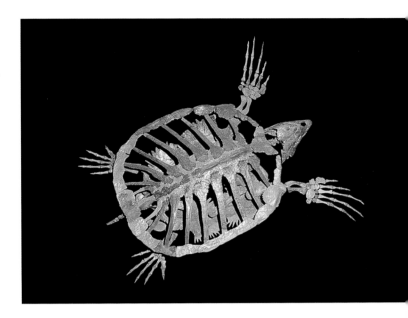

The giant sea turtle Protostega, *from the late Cretaceous period (80 to 70 million years ago), could grow as long as 14 feet (4.2 m). Most modern turtles have a solid bone layer in the carapace, but* Protostega, *like* Toxochelys, *had large gaps between the bones, which reduced the turtle's weight, possibly giving it an advantage in open sea habitat.*

3.3 feet (1 m) long. The turtle may have used its formidable curved beak to crush ammonites, shelled molluscs related to the chambered nautilus.

Many types of ammonites occupied the seas during most of the Mesozoic era, but they began to disappear toward the end of the Cretaceous period. This may explain why the protostegid turtles disappeared at about the same time. Only one species of protostegid is known to have survived the mass extinction that eliminated the dinosaurs and the last of the giant fish-like reptiles at the end of the Cretaceous period. Eventually it too disappeared, leaving the leatherback and cheloniid lines (and a variety of terrestrial and fresh-water turtles) to carry on to modern times.

CHAPTER 2

Between the Plates

ABOVE: The carapace scutes of green turtles, especially young ones, can be just as beautiful as those of the hawksbill, but they are thinner and much more difficult to work into decorative products.

LEFT: In this photograph, the hawksbill turtle's beautiful keratin tortoiseshell scutes, which cover the bone layer of its carapace, or upper shell, are clearly visible. The beauty of its shell proved to be the hawksbill's undoing. This turtle was photographed in the waters of the Cayman Islands—one of the few countries in the Caribbean that still permits a limited legal harvest of hawksbills.

The turtle's most obvious physical attribute is its shell. Other prehistoric reptiles developed similar shells, but for whatever reason did not survive and diversify in the way that turtles did. The shell, which in most turtles consists of two hard plates, protects the turtle's vulnerable body from predators, retards desiccation in dry environments, and can even allow the turtle to survive a fire. It can protect against trampling by grazing animals, serve as a weapon during competition for mates, or act as a digging tool when the turtle excavates burrows in which to rest. The shell is also a storehouse for the minerals that freshwater turtles need to survive a winter beneath the ice in frozen ponds. For sea turtles, the shell serves as a fairing, like those encasing racing motorcycles, to reduce drag as the turtle moves through the water.

The turtle's shell is composed of two parts: the upper shell, or carapace, rests on the turtle's back; and the lower shell, or plastron, covers its underside. The shell itself is a layered composite, yielding a high strength-to-weight ratio. The shell's inner layer is made up of bone plates, while the outer layer consists of plates made of keratin, the type of protein found in hair, fingernails, snake scales, bird feathers, and animal horns. These keratin plates, known as scutes, are equivalent to scales on other reptiles. Sea turtles (except leatherbacks) also have scales on the head, flippers, and other skin surfaces. The number and arrangement of the scutes on the shell and scales on the head are useful for identifying sea turtles by species, and even individuals within a species. The scutes that are important for species identification are labeled in the diagram on page 29.

The leatherback turtle, which, as you may recall, is in a family separate from all other sea turtles, has a carapace formed mostly of oily connective tissue that is covered with rubber-like skin. Embedded in the underside of the skin is a thin mosaic-like layer of thousands of tiny polygon-shaped bone plates. Baby leatherbacks are covered with tiny scales, but adults have naked leathery skin.

The ribbed design of the leatherback's carapace, which is similar to some boat hulls, may provide a hydrodynamic or stabilizing advantage as this open ocean behemoth traverses entire ocean basins and dives thousands of feet deep in its search for food. Pilot fish accompany this leatherback, which was photographed in the Azores Islands of the North Atlantic.

This green turtle hatchling has just entered the ocean and begun its life journey. Unlike newborn mammals, which require an extended period of parental care, learning, and development before they are able to fend for themselves, this tiny reptile is ready to face life's challenges with no help from its parents. Sea turtles depend more upon preprogrammed behaviors, and less upon learned responses than humans.

The foreflippers of sea turtles like this Hawaiian green function according to Bernoulli's Principle, which states that an increase in the speed of a fluid results in a decrease in its pressure. Water must accelerate to pass around the thick, front edge and curved, upper surface of the flipper, creating an area of low pressure in front of and above the fin relative to the thinner trailing edge and flatter underside. This low pressure pulls the turtle forward and upward.

The bony plates in the upper shell's underlayer are joined together and buttressed by the ribs and backbone, which are fused to the underside of the carapace. (Again, the leatherback is an exception. Its ribs and vertebrae lie just under the carapace, but are not integrated with it.) As with humans and other mammals, the ribs protect the turtle's internal organs such as the heart and lungs, but turtles are unusual in that their pelvic and shoulder bones are within the ribs as well.

The shoulder and hip girdles support fore and hind limbs that contain essentially the same bones found in our own limbs, including five digits. The bones are hidden inside flippers, which are strengthened and stiffened with fibrous connective tissue. The foreflippers and the toe bones inside of them are greatly elongated. The rear flippers are smaller and more flexible. Freshwater turtles swim primarily by kicking with their rear flippers. Sea turtles sometimes paddle with the rear flippers, but usually they hold the rear flippers behind them to use as rudders for steering. The rear flippers can also function like elevator fins on airplanes to trim the head up or down as the turtle moves forward.

Most of the propulsion comes from the foreflippers, which are shaped like airplane wings. When sea turtles swim, they flap the foreflippers up and down in a figure eight pattern, enabling them to "fly" through the water like a penguin. Leatherbacks pull their flippers back and down, rather than back and up like all other sea turtles. As the flippers are pulled forward, water flow over the flippers creates lift, just as airflow over an airplane wing lifts it and pulls it forward. When the sea turtle pushes the flippers back again, the flippers push against the resistance of the water to drive the turtle forward.

When females come ashore to nest, they use their flippers to haul themselves up the beach. They use their foreflippers to clear away a body pit and then, using the more flexible hind flippers, they excavate the egg chamber. Terrestrial and freshwater turtles have a claw at the end of each toe, but sea turtles have no more than two claws along the edge of each flipper. Leatherbacks have no flipper claws, while hawksbills and loggerheads have two on each flipper, and all other sea turtles have one claw per flipper. The forward claw on the foreflipper is longer and more curved in males, which use it as a hook to grasp the edge of the female's carapace during mating.

Although sea turtles belong to the "hidden neck" group of turtles, they cannot retract their heads inside their shells as other members of this group can. Perhaps to compensate for this inability, the skull bones of sea turtles are heavy and fused solid. Sea turtles do have openings for the eyes, ears, and nostrils, but the large openings found in the upper skull of other modern reptiles are missing. At one time, this led biologists to classify turtles with the extinct anapsids—the most primitive reptiles. Some biologists now believe that turtles are derived from the diapsid

Schematic dorsal view of a sea turtle

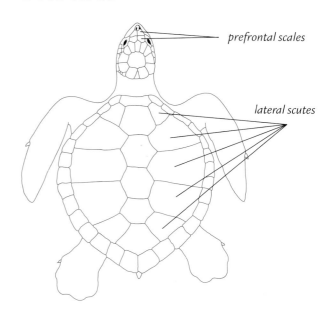

prefrontal scales

lateral scutes

Schematic generalized sea turtle skeleton

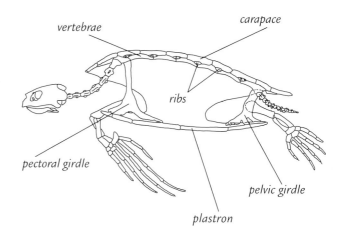

vertebrae

carapace

ribs

pectoral girdle

pelvic girdle

plastron

Because the locomotor and sensory systems of sea turtles are optimized for use underwater, the females are nearly helpless during that brief period of their lives when they must come ashore to lay their eggs. These olive ridleys in Costa Rica have only their size, their hard shells, and the "safety in numbers" principle to protect them from predators on land.

reptiles, which normally have two large holes in the upper skull, but have lost the holes, perhaps as an adaptation to aquatic living.

Turtles have no teeth, but the horny beak has a sharp edge capable of biting into or breaking open a variety of foodstuffs. In green turtles, the lower beak has tooth-like serrations. This may be an adaptation for snipping off blades of seagrass (adult green turtles are the only herbivorous sea turtles). Leatherbacks have a deep notch in the upper jaw corresponding to a sharp point on the lower beak—possibly an adaptation for feeding on jellyfish.

Internal Systems

In most aspects, the internal organs and physiology of sea turtles are similar to those of other reptiles. The saltwater environment, however, requires special adaptations, including the need to eliminate excess salt from the body. The seawater in which sea turtles live and the food they consume contain about three times as much salt as the turtle's own body fluids. Marine reptiles have developed a variety of ways to remove the excess salt from their bodies. Marine iguanas, for example, excrete salt through a gland in the nose, "sneezing" it out of their bodies. Estuarine crocodiles excrete salt through a gland on the tongue and eliminate it through the mouth. Sea turtles, however, excrete excess salt through their salt glands—evolutionarily modified tear glands—in the form of brine. Twice as salty as seawater, the brine "weeps" from their eyes. These salt glands are so important to the sea turtle's survival that they are the largest organs in the skull— many times larger than the tiny brain.

The lungs of sea turtles are quite different from other reptiles. Located on top of the turtle's body, just underneath the carapace, the lungs are reinforced with cartilage and elastic muscle tissue, and have large, stiff bronchial passageways. To obtain oxygen, sea turtles must draw air into their lungs with a few rapid breaths through the mouth. With each breath, a sea turtle can exchange 80 percent or more of the air in its lungs. This is a much higher percentage than other reptiles (or humans, who exchange only about 10 percent). The lungs of sea turtles are also much more efficient at

LEFT: Loggerhead turtles have two claws on the foreflipper. The forward claw, such as the one on this female, is large enough to serve as a defensive weapon. In males, the foreclaw is longer and more curved for use as a grappling hook.

BELOW: Hundreds of olive ridley turtles dig their nests in a black sand beach that is littered with the white shell fragments of unearthed eggs from earlier nesters.

transferring oxygen into the blood than most reptiles. Gas transfer between the blood and the lungs occurs only in the soft parts of the lung and not in the stiff passageways. During deep dives, the soft parts of the lungs collapse, forcing air into the rigid, nonabsorptive passageways. This helps sea turtles avoid a deadly condition known as "the bends" that occurs in human divers. Laboratory tests have shown that sea turtles can develop the bends from extreme dives, but it is not known to occur in nature.

After diving for half an hour or so, a sea turtle typically spends less than a minute at the surface before submerging again. During this time, it must take in all of the oxygen it needs for the next dive. Sea turtles may spend 96 percent or more of their time submerged. Typical dive times range from about ten minutes to longer than an hour. Dives as long as five hours have been recorded in the wild, but some of the longer dive records may represent failures of the measuring or transmitting equipment. In the laboratory, green turtles have survived for up to six hours without breathing. It can be said for certain that some sea turtles dive for as long as three hours under normal circumstances, and are capable of going without oxygen for longer.

Briny secretions twice as salty as seawater flow from the eyes of sea turtles to eliminate the excess salt they absorb from their environment. When females come ashore, like this olive ridley nesting in Costa Rica, they appear to have "tears" oozing from their eyes. Contrary to folklore that the turtles are crying because they will never see their babies, these tears have nothing to do with their emotional state.

Normally, turtles fuel their metabolism and activities with oxygen, like most other animals. When necessary, however, they can switch to anaerobic metabolism, which allows them to operate their bodies for hours without oxygen. Humans and other animals keep muscles operating with anaerobic metabolism when the ability of the blood to supply oxygen to the muscles has been exceeded. But in most vertebrates the ability of tissues to function temporarily without oxygen does not extend to the brain. If the brain is deprived of oxygen for more than a few minutes, death will result. Scientists have proven that loggerhead sea turtles and some freshwater turtles have the ability to reduce their brain function to a level that can be met by anaerobic metabolism. (Scientists have not yet studied all aquatic turtles, but it is likely that many have the same ability.) This apparently enables some freshwater turtles to hibernate under the ice throughout the winter. Turtles caught in trawl nets or otherwise forcibly held underwater, however, usually struggle and exceed the capacity of this system. They often drown in much less time than they might voluntarily dive.

The maximum depth to which sea turtles can dive is unknown. Only recently have scientists started to attach devices that can take these measurements. Green turtles can dive to at least 360 feet (110 m), loggerheads to at least 750 feet (230 m), and olive ridleys to at least 950 feet (290 m). Leatherbacks are among the deepest diving of all air-breathing animals, and can dive to more than 3,900 feet (1,200 m). Leatherbacks have the highest concentrations of red blood cells, hemoglobin, and myoglobin of any reptile. This enables them to store large amounts of oxygen in their blood and tissues—even more than in their lungs, which collapse when they dive. Shallow diving turtles, by contrast, keep air in their lungs while diving, and obtain most of their oxygen from their lungs while they are underwater.

Body Temperature and Range

In general, reptiles are considered to be "cold-blooded" or ectothermic, meaning that their body temperature varies with the external environment. To a certain extent, they are able to control their body temperature through their behavior. By moving from the shade into the sun, for example, reptiles can raise their body temperature. Green turtles sometimes crawl out of the water and lie on beaches or rocks for hours. Scientists speculate that these turtles may sometimes do this to

LEFT: Sea turtles, like this Hawaiian green, appear to have keen vision underwater. It is likely that eyesight is the sense they rely upon most when searching for food.

BELOW: Unlike fish, which can extract oxygen from seawater, turtles are reptiles and must come to the surface to breathe. Like this green turtle, they typically float horizontally at the surface and periodically lift the head to gasp air through the mouth before diving again.

RIGHT: These posthatchling leather-backs spent a few weeks in captivity, reaching a size where they are less vulnerable to predators, before they were released. (This is a controversial technique.) Researchers allow the turtles to crawl into the sea on their own, as many believe that baby turtles store (imprint) sensory information when they first enter the ocean that will help them find the nesting beach again when they mature years later.

BELOW: Green turtles are the only sea turtles known to leave the water for purposes other than nesting. This only occurs in a few locations, including the Galápagos Islands, where this group is basking. One possible function of this behavior is to raise body temperature, enabling digestion, egg maturation, and other body functions to proceed at a faster rate.

warm themselves, but that there may be other reasons for this behavior. Olive ridleys and loggerheads sometimes float at the surface for hours on calm days, probably to absorb the sun's heat through their exposed carapaces.

Green sea turtles, when swimming actively, may raise their body temperature as much as 14°F (8°C) above the water temperature. When inactive, however, green turtles, like loggerheads and olive ridleys, have a body temperature within 4°F (2°C) of the water temperature.

The need to keep body temperature within safe limits may affect many aspects of sea turtle behavior, especially nesting. Cold water temperatures can lead to cold stunning and death, while high temperatures, such as those a female might encounter if trapped on a hot beach after nesting, can cause overheating and death. For this reason, most sea turtles are limited to tropical and warm temperate seas and nest primarily at night. Leatherbacks, however, are able to migrate into cold, high-latitude seas and dive into cold waters. Like whales and other marine mammals, leatherbacks are insulated by a layer of fatty tissue under the skin, and have heat exchange mechanisms built into their circulatory system to protect against both chilling and overheating. They are able to maintain a body temperature at least 32°F (18°C) above that of the water in which they are swimming.

The Sensory Sea Turtle

Encased in the sea turtle's heavy skull is a small brain weighing only a fraction of an ounce (a few grams). One 230-pound (104 kg) green turtle, for example, had a brain weighing only 0.2 oz (6 g). This tiny neural computer, however, accomplishes remarkable feats and contains all the instructions a turtle needs to survive and navigate the ocean. The brain processes all the signals from the turtle's sensory organs.

Remarkably little is known about the sensory capabilities of sea turtles. In general, we can say that they have good color vision underwater, but are very nearsighted in air; have a good sense of smell; and can hear low frequency sounds. Somewhat surprisingly, sea turtles respond to being touched on the hard carapace, as well as on the softer parts of the body. Although they appear to prefer some foods to others, almost nothing is known about their sense of taste. It may not be very refined, as sea turtles often seem unable to distinguish food from nonfood items.

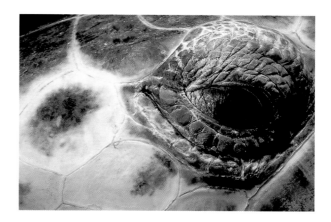

Eye of a loggerhead turtle.

By measuring the electrical response in the retina to exposure to light of different wavelengths, scientists have been able to determine that green turtles, at least, are most sensitive to light in the violet-blue-green-yellow part of the spectrum, and less sensitive to red and orange light, as might be expected for animals that live most of their lives in seawater, which absorbs red and orange light.

Sea turtles smell by pumping water in and out of the nostrils while underwater. The smell receptors are concentrated in two small areas—one on the upper surface of the nasal passageway and one on the lower surface. Separate trunks of the olfactory nerve connect the upper and lower receptors to different parts of the olfactory lobe of the brain. It is possible, then, that turtles have two different types of the sense of smell. The lower set of smell receptors may function as the Jacobsen's organ (the organ to which snakes touch their tongues when sampling the air) does in other reptiles. Scientists do not know if sea turtles are able to smell airborne odors, but some species have been known to push their beaks into the sand when coming ashore to nest, as if smelling the nesting beach. In a recent experiment, green turtles were best able to navigate to a small island from the downwind side of it.

The nostrils also provide an outlet through which sea turtles can expel water that enters the mouth while feeding. While the turtle is resting underwater, the nasal passages can be squeezed shut to keep water out. And, although sea turtles normally breathe by gasping air through their mouths as they surface, they sometimes breathe lightly through the nostrils when resting onshore.

A loggerhead turtle uses its foreflippers, or pectoral fins, in the same way a bird uses its wings to "fly" over the seafloor searching for food. The conch shells strewn across the bottom will become a food source when the turtle is larger and able to crush their thick shells with its beak.

The sea turtle's ears are entirely internal and encased in a bony capsule. There is no opening to the outside and no eardrum. Instead, the scaly skin covering the head functions as an eardrum. Sound is conducted to the ear from the skin via a layer of fat and two pieces of bone that function like our own ear bones. It is possible that sounds may also be received through the shell, and conducted to the head by the backbone. Turtles are most sensitive to low-frequency sounds and waterborne vibrations. Loggerhead and green turtles can hear sounds only up to a maximum frequency of about 800 Hz, and are most sensitive to sounds at about 200 Hz or below. (By comparison, humans have a hearing range from about 20 to 20,000 Hz.)

Sea turtles may use their low-frequency hearing for navigation. For example, by homing in on the characteristic sound of surf on a particular beach, female sea turtles may be able to find their way back to their nesting beach from the open ocean, or back to their feeding area after a breeding migration. Hatchlings can use the sound of the surf to find the ocean for the first time if no visual cues are available.

Sea turtles have at least one additional sense that we do not have—the magnetic sense. Many animals, from homing pigeons to sharks to bacteria, can orient themselves with respect to the earth's magnetic field. Tiny crystals of magnetite—which have been found in the brains of sea turtles and other migratory sea animals, including salmon, tuna, and whales—might explain this phenomenon. The magnetite may enable these animals to guide themselves just as a magnetized compass needle can guide a mariner.

Sea turtles, like these juvenile greens in Hawaii, may use the same resting areas on a daily basis. Where populations are reasonably dense, turtles may see and sometimes interact with the same other turtles every day over long periods of time. Some observers suggest that a social structure may develop among turtles that share a habitat.

Social Structure

In some species of sea turtles, a number of individuals may reside for many years within a small area, so there is a possibility for development of a social structure. Most scientists consider turtles to be solitary animals that do not engage in social relations apart from mating, but some researchers believe that a few species of sea turtles could be semi-social. Some have suggested that prior to massive exploitation by humans, green turtles might have traveled in large herds, similar to those of grazing animals on land. Some type of social facilitation appears to be at work in the mass nestings of ridley turtles, coordinating, for example, the near simultaneous emergence of dozens to hundreds of females from the sea. Sightings of "flotillas" of olive ridleys and Kemp's ridleys at sea suggest that they might migrate in groups. Mass migrations may have occurred in other species when they were more abundant. There have been a few reports of pairs of tagged females of various species repeatedly emerging to nest close together, nearly simultaneously, at intervals of two to three years. Small groups of olive ridleys also have been found nesting together in successive months. However, olive ridleys that nested together in groups were found to migrate to separate feeding areas afterwards, and green turtles that reside close together on their feeding grounds in Hawaii migrate separately to the breeding area. The possibility of long-term social bonds among sea turtles is intriguing, but without solid evidence at present.

CHAPTER 3

Mating Behavior and Reproduction

ABOVE: These eggs from the nest of a leatherback turtle show the range of sizes from a full-sized egg through various sizes of yolkless "duds."

LEFT: Like leatherbacks, green turtles use all four flippers together to propel themselves up a beach to a nesting site. Loggerheads, hawksbills, and ridleys alternate strokes of one front flipper in tandem with the rear flipper on the opposite side, while flatbacks use both types of gait. An expert would immediately identify this set of tracks on a Malaysian beach as having been made by a green turtle.

In the summertime, morning strollers along some Florida beaches are frequently baffled by meandering, parallel tractorlike tracks that appear in the sand. People are often quite surprised to learn that the tracks were made during the night by large, seagoing reptiles left over from the Age of Dinosaurs. Expert turtle watchers, on the other hand, know exactly what caused the strange tracks. In fact, by examining the tracks, many can identify the species of turtle that made them and can distinguish the incoming tracks from the exit tracks.

Over the course of more than one hundred million years of evolution, sea turtles have become exquisitely adapted to life at sea. But they remain tied to the land for the essential function of reproduction. After as long as half a century spent entirely at sea, roughly half of the sea turtles in the ocean (the females), haul themselves laboriously ashore to bury their eggs in the sand of a tropical or subtropical beach.

Sea turtles mate before the females lay the first clutch of eggs. The female stores the sperm internally, and can use it to fertilize all of the clutches that she lays in one season. Scientists believe that females rarely mate between a season's clutches. They may, however, mate with several males prior to laying the first clutch. Genetic tests have shown that a single clutch sometimes contains eggs fertilized by several different males. Mating can range from a tranquil interlude to a wild and violent melee.

While male turtles are known for their propensity to attempt to mount almost any suitably sized object in the water, it is also clear that they respond to females in reproductive condition, possibly by smelling pheromones that the female releases into the water. Males sometimes put their snouts right under the tails of females, as if "sniffing" them. During the brief courtship, males may circle, nuzzle, stroke, and nip at the female. The male may bite the female to subdue her as he attempts to climb on top of her. Females are frequently able to prevent unwelcome attempts at mounting, usually by adopting an upright posture and continually turning to face the male. If the male is able to get on top of the female, he grips the front edge of her carapace with the curved claws on his front

A female turtle (in the middle) mates with the male on top, as a second male underneath joins in and a third male approaches from the rear. Vigorous male competition helps to ensure that the strongest genes will be passed along to the next generation.

LEFT: In order to mate, the male turtle extends his long tail under the shell of the female so that the penis, located under his tail can enter the female's cloaca, which is under her shorter tail.

BELOW: A male green sea turtle (left) forcefully attempts to copulate with a female (right). The female resists by turning to face the male, preventing him from mounting her.

TOP: Especially when high tides occur late in the afternoon, female sea turtles, such as this green turtle, may come ashore to nest before night has fallen. Nesting during daylight hours usually occurs only in remote areas where the turtles are safe from human and animal predators, such as this small island in the Coral Sea off Australia.

RIGHT: A female olive ridley excavates the egg chamber of her nest on an arribada beach in Costa Rica. One rear flipper lifts out a scoop of sand. After dumping this scoop of sand, she will reach down with the other flipper to take the next scoop. She is surrounded by eggs and bits of eggshell from other nests that have been unearthed due to the density of nesting activity during arribadas.

flippers, wraps his elongated tail around the back of her carapace, and extends his penis from the underside of his tail into the genital opening on the underside of her shorter tail.

Once joined, the mating couple may stay in place for hours. The female has to do all the swimming, bringing both partners to the surface for air. At this time, the preoccupied turtles are vulnerable to attack by sharks, humans, and competing male turtles. One to eight or sometimes even more males may approach the couple and attempt to either dislodge the male or just join in. Sometimes they form a "pancake stack" with two or three males atop the female. Aggressive suitors may even bite the mounted male (or, more rarely, the female). A male may suffer such severe injuries to his tail and flippers during mating that he is unable to breed again for the rest of the season, assuring that other males will have a chance to contribute to the genetic diversity of that year's nesting effort.

Most sea turtles nest at night, reducing the possibility of lethal overheating and lessening the risk that daytime predators will find the nest and eat the eggs. In most populations of sea turtles, a few individuals nest in the late afternoon or early morning, but only the Kemp's ridley nests predominantly during the day. Olive ridley and Kemp's ridley sea turtles may nest either individually or in mass nestings called arribadas. Although olive ridleys nest mostly at night, the mass nestings often continue during both day and night.

Why do turtles nest on some beaches, and not on others? Many factors, which vary from species to species, appear to affect a female's selection of a nesting beach. Most importantly the nesting beach should be close to where the female herself hatched and entered the ocean. Other factors include accessibility from the ocean, beach slope and width, how high the tide rises on the beach, physical characteristics of the sand, amount of vegetation, presence of predators, beach development, and human activity (especially artificial lighting). Even after a turtle has crawled out of the ocean onto a particular beach, lights (especially moving lights); noises; obstacles; hard, compacted sand; or other impediments may cause the turtle to retreat to the sea without nesting, a behavior commonly known as a "false crawl." Sometimes a turtle makes one or more attempts at digging a nest before abandoning the effort. A turtle that makes a false crawl will usually emerge at a nearby location later that night or the next and lay her eggs.

Sea turtles use their flippers to haul themselves up the beach. Green and leatherback turtles use all four flippers together, while loggerheads, hawksbills, and ridleys alternate strokes of one front flipper in tandem with the rear flipper on the opposite side. Flatback turtles use both types of gait. Most turtles move up the beach intermittently, pausing every few feet until they are above the high tide line. A turtle may wander about the upper beach considerably, trying several sites before selecting a final nesting place. Then the turtle uses her front flippers to excavate a body pit slightly larger than the turtle's body, brushing away all the debris and loose, dry sand to expose moist sand in which an egg chamber will hold its shape without collapsing.

Sea turtles use the hind flippers to dig the egg chamber, alternating the left and right flippers, flex-

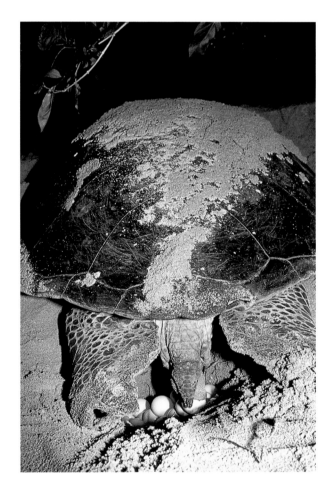

A female green turtle at the Turtle Islands Park in Malaysia drops eggs into the egg chamber through the ovipositor. When the female turtle is not laying eggs, the ovipositor is hidden inside the body.

ing to lift a scoop of sand and toss it aside. Although the turtle cannot see what she is doing, she expertly hollows out an elegant flask-shaped chamber with a long, narrow neck that leads to the larger, rounded compartment that will hold the eggs. The depth of the chamber depends upon the size of the turtle, or, more precisely, the length of her hind flippers. When the turtle is unable to extend her hind flippers any farther to scrape out more sand, she extends her ovipositor and begins to drop eggs into the nest.

The white, round, flexible eggs are about the size of ping-pong balls, but not as firm. The size and number of eggs laid vary from species to species and among populations and individuals of each species, generally averaging about 100 eggs. Flatbacks have fewer and larger eggs than most other species. The larger eggs produce larger hatchlings, which are less vulnerable to predation. Flatback hatchlings are believed to stay in coastal waters, rather than swimming immediately out to deep oceanic waters like other species of sea turtle. There are more predators in coastal waters, so the size advantage could be critical. Leatherbacks have the largest eggs of any sea turtle, commensurate with the large size of the parents, but egg-laying often concludes with the deposition of a number of smaller, yolkless eggs. Some green turtles also lay these yolkless "duds." Their function, if any, is unknown, but they may help to maintain the proper humidity or other characteristics of the nest environment, or possibly just eliminate excess egg-making material.

Much of the nesting process consists of instinctive, stereotyped behaviors, which the turtle does not

The eggs of the leatherback turtle are about the size of a racquet ball—considerably larger than the ping-pong-ball-sized eggs typical of most species of sea turtle. The eggs are quite flexible when laid, but as they develop they absorb moisture in the nest and become somewhat firmer.

alter in response to conditions. For example, a turtle with a partial hind flipper will alternate flipper movements while digging the nest cavity, even though only one flipper is actually moving sand. Nesting can be interrupted by a disturbance before the beginning of egg-laying, and sometimes during, but in general once the eggs begin to drop, the turtle will continue its routine regardless of activity around it. A turtle will usually continue to drop its eggs even as they are consumed by a predator or removed by a poacher, and will cover the nest in exactly the same fashion even if all the eggs have been removed.

After the last egg has dropped, the turtle uses its hind flippers to fill in the egg chamber and pack down sand over it. Ridley and flatback turtles also pound the sand over the nest with their plastrons. The turtle then flings sand with its front flippers to cover the body pit, both concealing the location of the nest, and providing the sand covering needed for proper incubation. The turtle moves forward as it is flinging sand, sometimes creating a false body pit, which may confuse some predators as to the location of the nest. Leatherbacks may make several false pits.

After covering the nest, the female turtle laboriously drags herself back down the beach, moving more quickly than on the way up, but still pausing to rest several times. She has now done all she can to ensure the survival of her offspring. Unlike some other animals, and even some reptiles, turtles play no part in raising their young. Either before or after plunging back into the water, leatherback turtles often loop around in one or more circles, possibly to orient themselves. Other turtles swim straight out to sea, but not too far. They will stay in the general area of the nesting beach until they have finished laying for the season.

During a nesting season, an individual female may lay anywhere from one to ten clutches of eggs. This varies from species to species, individual to individual, and season to season. The interval between nestings also varies between species and individuals, from an average of a week and a half in leatherbacks up to a month or more in ridleys. The time between successive nestings is less when the ocean is warmer, as higher temperatures allow the eggs to form faster within the turtle's body. After the last nesting of the season, the turtle leaves the area of the nesting beach to return to its feeding grounds. It will not return to nest again for a period of one to nine years or more, again varying among species and individuals. Most female sea

ABOVE: A hawksbill turtle flings sand over her nest after laying her eggs. Hawksbills tend to nest high up the beach and into the vegetation. Because they nest solitarily and throughout the year, their nesting is less predictable than other species and turtle watchers rarely see them.

LEFT: A green turtle returns to the sea at dawn after laying its eggs on the Malaysian island of Sipadan. As in many areas, game wardens will have to intervene to protect the nest from poachers, predators, and other threats. Development has accelerated erosion and debris accumulation, reducing the amount of beach available for nesting, so the nest will have to be moved to a hatchery where it will be safe from high tides and storm waves.

ABOVE: A monitor lizard feasts on the eggs of a green turtle on the island of Sipadan. Monitors are among the many wild, domestic, and feral animals that threaten sea turtle nests.

RIGHT: A near-term embryo of a Kemp's ridley sea turtle that died in the nest is well-developed, but it still has the yolk sac attached to its underside.

BELOW RIGHT: A Kemp's ridley hatchling emerges from its shell. Normally this would occur underground. This egg was dug out of a nest several days after the rest of the hatchlings had already surfaced and raced for the sea. It would have been unable to escape the nest on its own.

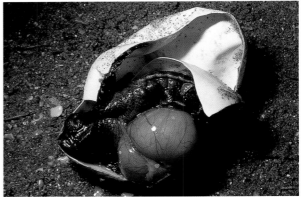

turtles make a nesting migration once every two or three years.

When the eggs are laid, the embryo inside consists of only a few cells. If all goes well, it will emerge a couple of months later as a self-sufficient organism capable of crossing the ocean and living for decades. For the first one to three days after the eggs are laid, the chance that predators will find the nest, either by smell or by visual clues, is great. Predators encompass a variety of wild, domestic, and feral animals, depending upon location. A partial list would include pigs, peccaries, dogs, dingos, foxes, coyotes, ants, maggots, beetles, raccoons, skunks, opossums, vultures and other birds, monitor lizards, iguanas, mongooses, coatis, jaguars, jaguaroundis, cats, rats, snakes, crabs, and humans. Some predators cannot actually reach the eggs without the help of others that excavate the nest first.

After a few days, the nesting odors dissipate and the wind usually covers the tracks and other disturbances to the sand. At this point, the eggs are relatively safe from predators until they hatch. There is still a chance that the nest can be destroyed by other nesting turtles, beach-cleaning machines, automobiles, high tides or surf, ground water, bacterial or fungal contamination, or desiccation.

The eggs absorb water and stiffen shortly after they are laid. In order for the embryos to survive, the moisture and humidity in the nest and gas exchange, which is governed largely by sand particle size, must be just right. The eggs hatch after an incubation period of one and a half to three months, depending upon the species and, more importantly, the temperature. A temperature increase of 14°F (8°C) can cut the incubation time in half. At temperatures below 73°F (23°C) or above 91°F (33°C) few of the eggs hatch.

The temperature has an even more interesting effect on the development of the embryos. The gender of sea turtles is not fixed genetically by the chromosomes, as it is in humans. Sea turtle embryos become female if the temperature stays above a "pivotal temperature" between 82 to 85°F (28–30°C) during the last third of the incubation period. The pivotal temperature varies depending upon species and location. At temperatures a little above the pivotal temperature,

the nest will be 100 percent (or nearly) female; a little below, and it will be 100 percent male.

Between these extremes, some of the hatchlings are female, and others are male. There is but a narrow margin (about 2°F or 1°C) between the extremes, so most nests produce predominantly one sex or the other. The temperature of the nest can be affected by many factors, including its specific placement on the beach and the time of year the eggs are laid. There is no evidence that females exert any deliberate control over the sex ratio of their offspring through nest placement or other means.

The fully developed embryos tear open their parchment-like eggshells with a tiny spike on the beak, known as an "egg-tooth" or caruncle. This "tooth," actually a hard projection of skin, disappears a few days after the embryos hatch. The first embryo to hatch is barely able to uncurl itself within the confines of the other eggs. As others hatch, the fluid inside their eggshells drains out the bottom of the nest, and the shells are flattened, creating space which enables the hatchlings to start squirming around. The movement of each hatchling stimulates the others. The thrashing of those at the top of the pile knocks sand down from the roof of the nest, while those at the bottom compact it, raising the floor. Through this "witless collaboration," as Archie Carr called it, the entire nest moves slowly upward. Predators can detect the sound of the wriggling hatchlings, and possibly the odor of the egg fluids, so at this point the baby turtles become vulnerable once again.

When the uppermost turtles encounter sand warmer than the nest, they stop moving. When the temperature of the sand above them drops, they begin digging again. This mechanism ensures that most hatchlings emerge at night, although some come out early in the morning, or on cool, cloudy or rainy afternoons. At the moment they burst through the surface of the sand, from one to seven days after hatching (usually two to three), the little turtles enter a period of intense danger. Facing odds much worse than those confronted by the soldiers landing in Normandy on D-Day, the tiny reptiles commence a great journey that will last many years and thousands of miles with a mad dash for survival across the beach to the sea.

CHAPTER 4

The Lost Decade

ABOVE: A hatchling green turtle emerges from the beach sand on the island of Sipadan, off the coast of Borneo.

LEFT: Upon reaching the ocean, Kemp's ridley hatchlings, like those of other sea turtles, swim quickly offshore to deep blue water. Kemp's hatchlings, however, do not appear to continue their swimming frenzy for as long as green or loggerhead turtles. They may also tend to hatch at a time and place where they are less likely to encounter currents that will carry them far away. As a result, most Kemp's ridleys remain in the Gulf of Mexico, unlike other species that may drift and swim across entire oceans as they develop.

A slight depression appears in the featureless sand of the beach and then out pops a tiny head, followed by a little scaly flipper. Soon the pit is boiling with hatchling sea turtles, scrambling over each other and flippering wildly down the beach toward the ocean. Those that stay on the beach will be killed by heat and desiccation if predators do not get to them first. All of the animals that eat turtle eggs also eat the hatchlings. On their way to the waves the hatchlings risk being snatched by ghost crabs or birds, which pose a threat both on the beach and in the water. The killing zone extends well beyond the surf line. Predatory fish, such as sharks, and sometimes dolphins, squid, and other animals, cue into the turtles' emergence and patrol the beach. It is not until the hatchlings reach the open ocean that they attain any degree of relative safety.

When they first emerge from the nest, the hatchlings may not be able to see the water. Yet, unless confused by artificial stimuli, they usually begin to move directly toward the ocean. The tiny turtles figure out the direction of the ocean in one of three ways. On a natural beach, vegetation and dunes tend to create dark silhouettes on the landward horizon, while the reflection of starlight and moonlight creates a brighter horizon on the seaward side. Hatchling turtles ignore the sky overhead and concentrate on the horizon, moving away from any dark silhouettes and toward the brightest portion of the horizon. When artificial lighting and/or the clearing of dunes and vegetation reverse the natural lighting ratio on the beach, the results can be disastrous. In the absence of visual cues, hatchlings will move down a slope. If there

Hatchling Kemp's ridley turtles emerge from a nest in a hatchery at the turtle camp at Rancho Nuevo, Mexico. The combined efforts of the hatchlings are necessary for them to rise upward through the sand to the surface.

Hatchling green sea turtles scramble down the slope of a beach in the Turtle Islands of Malaysia. On average, only one hatchling from a nest of about 100 will survive the first year, and only one in 1,000 will survive to adulthood and return to reproduce in the same area.

is neither a slope nor visual cues, hatchlings will move toward the sound of the surf.

When the little turtles reach the ocean, their first contact is usually with a rush of foam from a breaking wave that pushes them back up the beach. Initially they must swim directly against this powerful surge, then, as the backwash pulls them out, they must swim with it before diving beneath the next approaching wave. Buffeted by violent surge forces in the dark of night, the hatchlings must quickly escape the churning surf, or risk being thrown back onto the beach. No longer able to see the horizon, they orient themselves using built-in biological accelerometers. As a wave approaches the beach, objects in the water are moved in a circular path. An object is lifted upward, pushed toward the beach, carried downward, and then pulled away from the beach by the undertow. By monitoring the acceleration of its body in different directions, a hatchling can orient itself to face the waves and swim away from the beach.

This strategy works in very shallow water because waves are refracted by the sea bottom as they approach the shore, arriving at the shoreline head on. Only a few yards out to sea, however, the waves may be moving in almost any direction. Yet the hatchling must continue to swim away from the shoreline as fast as possible if it is to survive. Any number of fish, birds,

Loggerhead sea turtle hatchlings emerge from the sand at dawn and head for the ocean. Once above ground, each hatchling must rapidly assess its surroundings, establish its position relative to the shoreline, set a course that will guide it to open ocean, and make a run for its life. Scientists have only recently begun to understand how the little turtles accomplish this.

A loggerhead hatchling in Florida nears the water. Only the fastest, strongest, and luckiest hatchlings will make it past the gauntlet of predators on the beach and in the ocean near shore. This is the ultimate biathlon competition, and only the top 1 percent survive.

and other animals that are abundant close to shore will devour baby sea turtles.

A turtle hatchling is about the size of a small mouse. It is only able to lift its head an inch or so above the surface of the water and waves block its view. Its own buoyancy prevents a hatchling from diving more than a few yards; therefore it cannot see the seafloor. So how do the hatchlings find their way? Laboratory experiments have shown that sea turtles can detect the magnetic field of the earth. After establishing a course of travel from cues such as brightness of the horizon or wave action at the shoreline, the hatchlings switch to magnetic guidance to maintain the same course as they continue out to sea.

In some parts of the world, hatchlings enter the sea from beaches where there are no waves, and from beaches that do not face out toward open sea. Yet somehow when they reach the water they are able to swim away from the beach and then establish a course that will carry them out to sea. They are even able to navigate around reefs and islands blocking their path. How sea turtle hatchlings accomplish this remains unknown.

The "frenzy"—the frantic nonstop crawling/swimming action that characterizes newlyhatched sea turtles—lasts about twenty-four hours in green, loggerhead, and leatherback turtles. The duration of the frenzy in other species is not yet known, but there are indications that it may be much shorter in flatback, Kemp's ridley, and hawksbill turtles—perhaps as short as two hours in the hawksbill. During its first couple of days in the ocean, the hatchling does not feed. The remainder of the egg yolk, which is carried in the turtle's abdominal cavity, fuels the near-constant activity. This rapid migration takes the hatchling offshore to the pelagic environment, where it begins the period of its life known as the pelagic phase or developmental migration.

The flatback turtle and perhaps some hawksbill turtles appear not to have a pelagic phase. Available evidence indicates that flatback turtles stay in nearshore waters throughout their lives, rarely entering waters deeper than about 150 feet (45 m) as juveniles or adults. Leatherback turtles, on the other hand, spend their entire lives (apart from the reproductive phase) in pelagic habitat. After entering the ocean, the hatchlings swim offshore for at least six days and are not seen again for four years or longer. Little is known about where they go. Some (but not all) olive ridleys,

may also spend their whole lives in open ocean, while some (but not most) hawksbills may never leave coastal waters. For other sea turtles, the pelagic phase encompasses a distinct period of their lives—a time when feeding, sleeping, and migratory habits are markedly different from those they will adopt once they return to coastal waters. During this period, the young turtles are rarely seen by humans. Until recently, where baby turtles go between the time they leave the beach with shells roughly the size of the bowl of a spoon, and when they are again seen close to shore with shells that are dinner plate size or larger, was a great mystery. Biologists called this period the "lost year." We now know that this time frame usually lasts much longer than a year.

A black vulture snatches up an olive ridley hatchling that was washed back onto a Costa Rican beach by a wave. There will be no second chance for this baby turtle. Unlike humans, who are protected by their parents for years as they gain survival skills, sea turtles must begin their lives with impressive physical and navigational abilities or be quickly eliminated from the population.

The duration of the "lost year" varies dramatically among species of sea turtles, different populations of a species, and different individuals within a population. The pelagic phase is estimated to last between one and ten years for most sea turtles. Sea turtles that live in the Pacific Ocean tend to have a longer pelagic phase than sea turtles that live in the Atlantic.

During the first part of the pelagic phase, loggerhead and hawksbill hatchlings often seek out floating patches of sargassum and other types of seaweed, where they can hide from predators. They feed on small shrimps, crabs, snails, worms, insects, fish, and other organisms that live in the weed, and on sea jellies and other creatures that float by. Kemp's ridley and olive ridley hatchlings probably do the same. Green and leatherback turtles, however, are believed to prefer open water, where they likely consume larger amounts of small sea jellies and other organisms that float in open surface waters. Green turtle hatchlings have been found in sargassum at least twice, but may have been pushed into it by converging currents. In laboratory experiments, loggerhead and hawksbill hatchlings were attracted to floating artificial weedbeds, while green turtle hatchlings avoided them. When threatened, the baby green turtles tended to dive and swim away, while the loggerheads and hawksbills remained motionless—a good strategy if hidden in seaweed.

Predators and scavengers on the nesting beaches, such as this ghost crab in Florida, quickly take advantage of any weak, dead, or dying turtle hatchlings left behind in the rush to the sea. Crabs sometimes burrow into turtle nests and attack the eggs before they hatch.

These ecological differences are reflected in the coloring of the baby turtles. Green, leatherback, and flatback hatchlings sport a two-tone pattern that biologists call countershading. A dark carapace helps the turtle blend into the dark waters of the open ocean when viewed from above, while a white plastron renders the hatchling less visible when seen from below against a background of sky and clouds. Ridley, loggerhead, and hawksbill hatchlings, on the other hand, are a uniform brown to gray color, which may help them blend into a patch of floating weed. Predation levels are very high on these small turtles, so a camouflage pattern that matches their habitat is crucial to their survival. Floating seaweed, however, is common in the Atlantic, but too rare in the Pacific to provide dependable habitat.

From captures by sea eagles and shrimp trawls we know that juvenile flatbacks are usually found within 100 miles (150 km) of a nesting beach. In other species of sea turtles, the juveniles are likely to be found hundreds to thousands of miles from the beach where they hatched.

Although the pelagic periods of sea turtles are not well known, scientists have been able to work out the basics of the developmental migrations of loggerheads. From these findings, they have been able to extrapolate what the pelagic stage might be like for other sea turtles. Loggerheads make one of the most phenomenal migrations in the animal kingdom. Loggerheads that hatch in Japan traverse the Pacific, spending time off the coast of Mexico, where they feed on aggregations of pelagic red crabs, before they return to Japan. One turtle that was tagged and released off the coast of Mexico was caught a little more than a year later in a net in Japan, 6,500 miles (10,600 km) away. During the developmental migration, these turtles travel a minimum of 12,400 miles (20,000 km) and they probably often travel much farther!

Loggerhead turtles hatched on the southeast coast of North America enter the North Atlantic Gyre, a huge current system that spins clockwise around the entire North Atlantic. The great Gulf Stream current sweeps north along the east coast of North America to Newfoundland, where it heads east and crosses the Atlantic as the North Atlantic Current. About two-thirds of the way across the Atlantic, near the Azores Islands, the current splits into the North Atlantic Drift, which flows northeast toward the British Isles, and the Canary Current, which flows south, past the Madeira Islands. Somewhere near the Canary Islands,

Starting out on its grand voyage from the nesting beach to the open ocean, this green turtle hatchling is clad in "tuxedo colors" with a dark carapace and light plastron—seemingly an ideal pattern for an open ocean existence. In at least some green turtles, however, the plastron turns from light to dark and back to light again as the young turtle grows. As almost nothing is known about the green turtle's habits during the pelagic phase, it is hard to guess what purpose this change in coloration might serve.

BOTH PHOTOS: A leatherback turtle hatchling swims in open ocean off the nesting beach. For the next several years, its life will be a mystery. Unlike adult leatherbacks, the hatchling's body is covered with small scales.

which are located off the coast of North Africa, the current turns westward to cross the Atlantic again as the North Equatorial Current.

Turtles that manage to stay within this gyre are able to successfully complete their developmental migration and return to North America to begin the bottom-dwelling phase of their lives. Those that, for example, are caught in the North Atlantic Drift and swept up to Britain usually die from the cold. The turtles can avoid being transported out of the gyre by swimming, but to choose the right direction, they must know where they are.

Scientists have determined that baby loggerheads are able to detect both the strength and angle of magnetic force-field lines. Since the combination of these characteristics varies throughout the earth's magnetic field, it is theoretically possible for turtles to carry an internal map and compass that could guide them to any place on the earth. A map sense has not been proven, but it has been shown that baby Florida loggerheads, when exposed in the lab to magnetic fields replicating the fields at specific locations in the North Atlantic, tend to swim in directions that would keep them within the gyre. The ability to sense magnetic fields, however, does not by itself explain the amazing navigational abilities of sea turtles.

The pelagic phase of North Atlantic loggerheads is believed to last three to fifteen years. Some of the turtles wander into the Mediterranean for awhile. Many of the turtles spend several of these years floating around the Azores and Madeira Islands. Although there appears to be very little life in these clear, blue oceanic surface waters, scientists believe that the small turtles are able to locate areas where currents converge and sea jellies and other animals accumulate. As the turtles grow, they are better able to dive for food below the surface.

Almost nothing is known about the return migration to the western Atlantic, but when they reach a

A loggerhead hatchling off Florida takes refuge in a clump of sargassum (a type of brown algae) floating at the sea surface. The sargassum provides more than just a hiding place from predators—it also serves as a rich hunting ground for small shrimp, fish, and other organisms that cling to the fronds. Floating seaweed is much less common in the Pacific Ocean than the Atlantic, so the developmental habitat of hatchlings in the Pacific remains somewhat mysterious.

carapace length of 10 to 33 inches (25–84 cm), loggerheads begin to show up as bottom-dwellers along the coast of North America from Cape Cod, Massachusetts, to southern Texas. Some of them may spin around the North Atlantic more than once before settling down. Some apparently move back and forth between the coastal and pelagic habitats for awhile, and even mature loggerheads may make trips offshore to feed at oceanic "fronts" where water masses converge. Most loggerheads, however, stick mostly to bottom feeding from the time they reach a shell length of about half a yard in the Atlantic, and a little less than a yard in the Pacific.

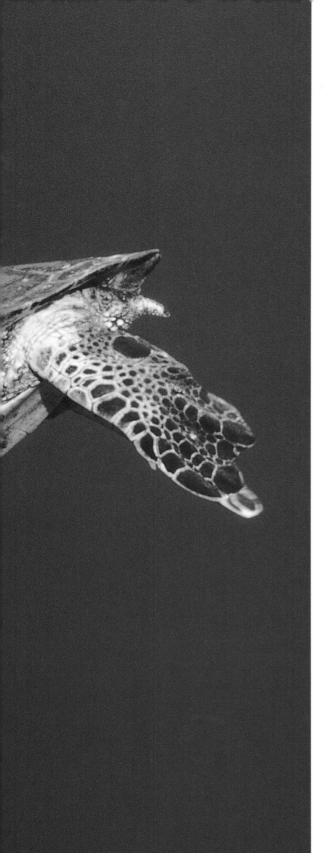

CHAPTER 5

Growing Up

ABOVE: A hawksbill turtle in Thailand forages on a seamount festooned with colorful soft corals. Of all sea turtles, hawksbills are the most closely tied to the coral reef habitat, although it is not unusual to see other species of sea turtles, especially green turtles, on coral reefs. The acorn barnacles studding the plastron of this turtle belong to a species found only on sea turtles.

LEFT: This juvenile green turtle in Hawaii has already returned from the pelagic zone to coastal habitat and begun to feed primarily on plants, but it will still take an easy meal of a sea jelly if the opportunity presents itself.

During the mysterious pelagic phase, the small turtle develops from a hatchling (that is still living off the yolk mass in its gut) to a posthatchling (not much larger than a hatchling, but starting to capture its own food) to a juvenile (a turtle of any size that is not yet sexually mature). In leatherback turtles, and possibly some olive ridleys, the entire juvenile period of development and the adult stage is spent in the pelagic environment. Very little is known about the juvenile phase of leatherbacks. The turtles essentially disappear from the time the hatchlings enter the water until mature females crawl back on the beach to nest. Large juveniles are occasionally seen at sea or wash ashore dead, but small juveniles are almost unknown. Scientists know very little about the juvenile stage of olive ridley and flatback turtles also. These turtles, too, may not have a juvenile phase that is clearly distinguished from their adult lives.

The juvenile life of the remaining four species of sea turtles is somewhat better known. These species spend the first part of their juvenile period in the pelagic stage, then begin the "benthic immature" stage of their lives with a move inshore and a shift in diet from pelagic to primarily bottom-dwelling organisms. These small turtles still come to the surface to breathe, but after filling their lungs, they dive to the bottom to rest or search for food. At night they sleep wedged into some bottom structure, such as a rock or shipwreck, instead of floating on the surface.

The size and age at which the young turtle begins the bottom-dwelling or benthic phase of its life varies among individuals, species, and oceans. Scientists generally believe that this stage begins at a greater size and age in the Pacific, where the pelagic developmental migration lasts longer than in the Atlantic. In the Atlantic, the benthic immature stage usually begins at a shell length between 8 to 10 inches (20–25 cm) for hawksbill and Kemp's ridley turtles, 10 to 14 inches (25–35 cm) for green turtles, and 16 to 25 inches (40–64 cm) for loggerheads. In the Pacific, greens and

Loggerhead turtles, such as this one in the Bahamas, are very fond of spiny lobsters. In Florida, fishermen complain that loggerheads sometimes demolish lobster traps and crab traps to get at the crustaceans inside. Loggerheads also prey heavily on molluscs. Their diet composition changes as they grow and develop more powerful jaws, which are capable of crushing heavier shells.

ABOVE: A green sea turtle feeds on green algae in the Galápagos Islands. In habitats where seagrasses are not available, green turtles can subsist entirely on algae.

LEFT: Shipwrecks, like this one in the Bahamas, often attract loggerhead turtles, which return to the wrecks each night to sleep. A sharksucker (remora) has attached to this loggerhead's carapace using the suction pad on top of its head.

hawksbills usually enter this stage at a size of about 14 inches (35 cm) or larger, and loggerheads at 28 inches (70 cm) or more.

Most sea turtles tend to select certain sections of the seafloor as their homes for long periods of time—sometimes many years. As they grow, turtles may move through a series of "developmental habitats." Some of these habitats are occupied seasonally. Examples of seasonally used developmental habitats include Long Island Sound and Chesapeake Bay on the northeast coast of the United States. Large numbers of juvenile loggerhead, green, and Kemp's ridley turtles spend the summer months in these shallow bodies of water. In the winter, these turtles migrate south to warmer waters along the southeastern coast of the United States. Some turtles that feed in shallow bays during the summer migrate offshore to deeper waters in winter, where they will not risk death when a cold front passes over very shallow water, causing a rapid drop in water temperature. In some cases, the juvenile habitat may be far from the adult habitat. In other instances, juveniles share the adult habitat.

The duration of the benthic immature stage varies tremendously—not only among species and local populations, but also among individuals within a population. It can be as short as five years, or, in rare cases, last more than sixty years. Once they reach maturity, most turtles will begin a pattern of migrating

One animal's waste can be another animal's feast. The batfish (spadefish) following this green turtle in Malaysia values the turtle's feces so highly that it will attempt to drive away any other batfish that approaches.

every few years between their feeding habitat and their breeding area. While in the feeding habitat, however, many turtles occupy very restricted areas, particularly when it comes to a choice of resting and sleeping places. An individual can often be regularly found resting under a particular rock, coral head, or shipwreck. In experiments, sea turtles removed from their feeding territories and released 60 miles (100 km) or more away usually find their way back in a short time. On the contrary, leatherbacks and olive ridleys appear to be largely nomadic or semi-nomadic, moving about to take advantage of seasonal or temporarily abundant food resources.

The progression through developmental habitats probably corresponds with shifts in diet composition as the turtle grows. We know very little about these shifts, however. In most cases, the diet of large juveniles is probably similar to the diet of adults. The biggest shift in diet occurs when the turtle settles to the bottom after its pelagic phase.

For the green turtle, this is a huge change. The pelagic juveniles, like those of other species, are mostly carnivorous, but when they settle to the bottom, they switch to a vegetarian diet. All other sea turtles remain mostly carnivorous throughout their lives, eating jellies, sponges, crabs, or other animals. Sea turtles of different species may live in close proximity to one another, but minimize competition by utilizing different portions of the habitat and seeking different prey. In Chesapeake Bay, for example, juvenile Kemp's ridleys feed on blue crabs in shallow grass flats, while immature loggerheads feed in deeper channels where they capture horseshoe crabs. Green turtles sharing the same bay eat only seagrasses and algae.

As far as we know, most sea turtles—except some populations of green turtles—feed primarily by day and sleep at night. When not feeding or migrating, sea turtles spend much of their time resting. Most often, a turtle will find a protected area, such as an underwater cave or ledge, in which to rest. Sometimes turtles, particularly olive ridleys and loggerheads, rest while floating at the surface. This behavior is called "basking," based on the belief that the purpose is to absorb heat from the sun in order to raise the turtle's body temperature. This probably is the primary purpose of surface basking, which usually occurs around midday in calm weather, and often in cool water. In certain areas, such as the Galápagos and Hawaiian Islands,

Two creatures with similar odd diets share a symbiotic relationship. Angelfish and hawksbill turtles are among the few animals known to feed primarily on sponges. Because angelfish prefer the inner tissues of sponges, they often follow hawksbills, which are better able to bite through the outer covering of sponges, and feed in the openings breached by the turtles. A Spanish hogfish wrasse hovers in the background, hoping to snatch any shrimp, worms, or other small creatures that are dislodged as the turtle feeds.

LEFT: Two hawksbills face off on a reef on Sipadan Island, Malaysia. A hawksbill will usually challenge any other hawksbill it finds feeding in its territory. The matter is usually settled without violence when one turtle leaves.

ABOVE: Underwater photographs of the Kemp's ridley turtle are quite rare. This species is critically endangered, occurs almost exclusively in the Gulf of Mexico (as an adult), and does not frequent the coral reefs and clear waters favored by scuba divers.

FACING PAGE: A hawksbill turtle cruises over a coral reef at Layang Layang Atoll in the South China Sea. Although the sponges that form the basis of the hawksbill's diet are not nearly as prominent on reefs in the Indo-Pacific region as they are in the Caribbean, hawksbills can still find plenty of nourishment by gnawing encrusting sponges off the undersides of corals.

green sea turtles bask on shore. Adjusting body temperature is probably only one of several reasons why these turtles come out of the water to rest. At breeding beaches, females appear to bask as a way to escape the attentions of amorous males. In places where there are no predators on land but tiger sharks are common in the water, sea turtles may rest in safety on beaches close to the prime feeding areas while waiting for a favorable tide in which to feed in shallow water. It may also be more energy-efficient to rest on shore, where the turtle can breathe at will, rather than building up an oxygen debt and having to wake up to swim to the surface every so often. Basking in the sun may additionally be a way to kill or weaken parasites or encrusting organisms that cling to the turtle's skin and shell.

By the time they return from their open ocean sojourn to the nearshore environment, sea turtles are large enough to be safe from most of the predators they will encounter there. However, they are still subject to attack by large fishes, such as sharks and giant groupers. In some areas, when they come very close to shore, some sea turtles may be attacked by crocodiles. Crocodiles, coyotes, dogs, jaguars, tigers, and hyenas can also threaten females on nesting beaches. As turtles grow, the number of animals able to threaten them decreases. However, even the largest sea turtle, a full-grown, thousand-pound (450 kg) leatherback, can be torn apart and eaten by an orca (killer whale). While many types of sharks consume hatchlings, only a few species, adapted for dismembering large prey, pose a threat to an adult or large juvenile sea turtle. Great white sharks, bull sharks, and oceanic whitetip sharks occasionally take sea turtles, but only tiger sharks consume adult turtles with any frequency. Scientists believe that the tiger shark's cockscomb-shaped teeth have adapted over time to be able to saw through the shells of sea turtles.

Turtles are often able to ward off attacks by turning the broad side of the carapace toward the threat, presenting the attacker with a target that is too wide to get into its mouth. A leatherback turtle was filmed successfully avoiding a tiger shark attack by flipping

Green sea turtles regularly come ashore to bask on certain beaches in Hawaii. This behavior may have been common in many areas without terrestrial predators before humans arrived. Initially, turtles were believed to bask mainly to absorb heat from the sun. This turtle, however, came out of the water shortly before sunset and stayed on the beach for a good part of the night.

ABOVE: This green turtle on Sipadan Island has survived a massive shark bite, and is fully functional. The bite appears to have occurred when the turtle was smaller and to have grown with the turtle.

LEFT: A green sea turtle in Hawaii has large turtle barnacles attached to its plastron. One reason that green turtles often spend a lot of time rubbing their shells against coral heads and other hard objects may be to dislodge barnacles. The barnacles certainly create drag and have a negative effect on the turtle's hydrodynamics. Some experts believe, however, that such barnacles may function like armor, possibly giving the turtles an advantage in areas where tiger sharks or other large predatory sharks are abundant.

RIGHT: This juvenile loggerhead, with its carapace nearly covered by stalked gooseneck barnacles, was almost moribund when collected off the Azores Islands in the North Atlantic. It may be that the burden of dragging the barnacles through the water sapped the turtle's energy, or slowed it down so that it was unable to catch food as effectively. It's also possible that the barnacles were able to easily settle and attach themselves on the turtle's shell because the turtle was already unhealthy and inactive. It could well be that both scenarios are true, and they reinforce each other in a vicious cycle.

BELOW: Two large sharksuckers (remoras) have attached themselves to the plastron of a loggerhead turtle in the Bahamas. With their suckers on top of their heads, they are able to ride right-side-up when attached underneath the turtle. When attached to the carapace, they ride in an upside-down position, which does not appear to bother them in the least.

FACING PAGE: At a cleaning station in Hawaii, yellow tangs and gold ring surgeonfish have descended onto the carapace of a green turtle to eat the algae that has grown on it. The turtle is gliding slowly with its flippers drooping, an invitation for the cleaner fish to jump aboard.

Sailfin tangs clean algae from the shell of a hawksbill turtle in the Maldive Islands. While green turtles and hawksbills are the only sea turtles regularly seen by divers at cleaning stations, it is likely that other species of sea turtles utilize the services of cleaner fish as well.

upside down at the surface when the shark approached, then diving behind the shark and biting it. In another filmed sequence, a loggerhead turtle turned on a tiger shark during a chase and bit it on the gills, driving it away. Most successful shark attacks are surprise attacks from the rear, which sometimes leave the turtle with part of a flipper or shell missing.

Smaller enemies such as leeches, flukes, and other external and internal parasites also attack sea turtles. Turtles are susceptible to great variety of diseases too. In recent years, some diseases, notably fibropapilloma, or FP disease, have become much more prevalent, killing large numbers of turtles. Barnacles and algae attach to turtles, and, although they do not feed on the turtle as parasites and disease organisms do, they can impact the turtle's health by increasing water resistance when it swims, requiring the turtle to expend more energy. Green turtles are often seen rubbing their shells against rocks or coral heads. This may be a way of removing barnacles and other growths. More than 100 kinds of animals and plants are known to grow on loggerheads. Other creatures, such as pilot fish and other small fishes, sometimes accompany turtles without harming them. These fish are looking for protection from predators, and perhaps they are also conserving energy by gliding on the pressure wave produced by the swimming turtle. Remoras, or sharksuckers, often attach to larger turtles for a free ride. In parts of Asia, batfish often follow green turtles, rushing under the turtle when it defecates, to consume its feces.

More than 80 percent of juvenile loggerheads in the North Atlantic carry "hitchhikers" in the form of small Columbus crabs. Most of these crabs travel in male/female pairs and live at the base of the turtle's tail. In return for a secure mobile home, the crabs provide a valuable service—they eat small barnacles and parasites from the turtle's shell and skin. If left to grow, gooseneck barnacles can cover a turtle's shell like a mop and greatly increase the energy required for swimming. The crabs also cannibalize additional members of their own species that try to colonize the turtle.

Green turtles and hawksbill turtles are also known to enlist the help of other creatures to keep their skin

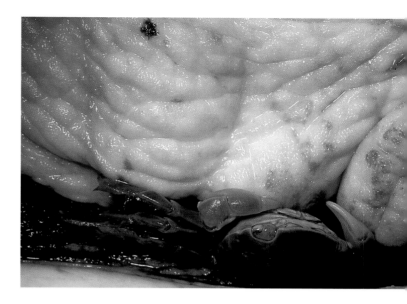

A Columbus crab nestles under the tail of a juvenile loggerhead in the Azores. Columbus crabs also live on inanimate floating objects, but those that live on turtles are larger and carry more eggs than those on inanimate objects, indicating that there is some benefit to living on a turtle.

and shells clean. For this service, the turtles usually go to specific locations on the reef where the cleaner fish live. Most of the known cleaner fish are surgeonfish, which are herbivorous (plant eaters). They swarm around the turtle and pick algae off its skin and shell. Small carnivorous fish, such as wrasses and pufferfish, may also attend the turtle, picking off parasites or bits of diseased or injured tissue. Upon entering the cleaning station, a turtle often adopts a specific pose or swims in a particular pattern to indicate its desire to be cleaned. A turtle perched high on its flippers with its neck outstretched is usually inviting cleaner fish to go to work.

At some of these cleaning stations, up to a dozen turtles sometimes gather and compete for the services of the cleaner fish. Turtles have been known to "steal" cleaners by settling on top of another turtle as it is being cleaned. These cleaning station areas are sometimes used as resting places. Certain turtles lay claim to particular spots on the bottom, displacing other turtles that attempt to use them.

CHAPTER 6

The Incredible Journey

ABOVE: The long, swollen tail on this mature male green sea turtle at Sipadan Island, Malaysia, is typical of a male in mating condition.

LEFT: A pair of loggerhead turtles mate in the Bahamas. The female (underneath) must swim for both turtles, as the male must use the claws on his foreflippers to grasp the leading edge of the female's carapace. Photo © Marilyn Kazmers / Seapics.com.

After many years of growth during the juvenile stages, remarkable changes take place in the sea turtle's life when it finally reaches adulthood. Externally, the changes are not very dramatic. The male turtle's tail begins to elongate, eventually extending well beyond the margin of the shell. The front flipper claws grow longer and more curved. Females show no obvious signs of the onset of maturity. In both sexes, however, changes occur internally. The reproductive organs begin to produce either sperm or eggs, and changes in the hormones coursing through the bloodstream prompt new behaviors, including some of the most incredible migrations in the animal kingdom.

The age at which sea turtles reach sexual maturity is very difficult to fix precisely, yet it is critical to understanding the life histories of sea turtles and to all efforts to conserve them. Among the most revolutionary advances in our knowledge of sea turtle biology over the past twenty-five years have been the new estimations of the age at which they begin to reproduce. In the 1960s scientists thought sea turtles began to reproduce at around six years of age. Now they have shown that most sea turtles do not begin to breed until much later in life and that the age of reproduc-

tion varies greatly by individual and by the region in which the turtle lives.

Scientists believe, for example, that Kemp's ridley turtles reach sexual maturity between the ages of seven and sixteen years. Loggerheads, on the other hand, do not normally begin to reproduce until they are between twenty and sixty years of age. After maturity, growth slows tremendously, leading to an interesting anomaly. Researchers used to assume that the largest females on the nesting beach were the oldest turtles. However, they now recognize that these are fast-growing turtles that reach a large size quickly, before they attain sexual maturity and stop growing. The smallest breeding females are now believed to be the oldest and slowest-growing individuals.

Once sexually mature, turtles embark on a new pattern of migration. For some sea turtles, this will be the third type of migratory pattern (the first two being the posthatchling developmental migration and the seasonal migrations between feeding grounds). With fairly few exceptions, turtles do not feed and breed in the same area. Instead they migrate to nesting beaches that may be as far as thousands of miles from their feeding grounds. Sea turtles usually target these breeding areas with great precision. Some green turtles that feed off the coast of Brazil, for example, breed at the tiny island of Ascension, a mere speck in the middle of the Atlantic. In many cases, female turtles faithfully nest within a few hundred yards of where they nested in previous years. Most sea turtles use the same breeding area throughout their adult lives.

Female turtles rarely make breeding migrations in successive years. Due to the amount of energy required to produce several clutches of eggs and complete a long journey (possibly without feeding for several months if food is not available in the breeding area), they usually feed for two or more years between nesting bouts. The length of time between breeding migrations varies tremendously, but on average, most females breed every two to three years. Much less is known about male turtles, however. They generally also migrate to the nesting areas, and mate with the females offshore.

Scientists Laura Sarti and Dr. Scott Eckert attach a satellite transmitter to a leatherback turtle nesting on the western coast of Mexico. Using this technology, Sarti and Eckert were able to determine that leatherbacks from this population follow a well-defined migratory path when they leave the nesting beach for their foraging grounds in the Southern Ocean. The population was decimated by gill nets and longlines set to catch swordfish off the coast of South America.

Navigation

The migration of sea turtles from their feeding grounds to distant nesting beaches raises several difficult questions that biologists have puzzled over for decades. One of the most fascinating mysteries is how the turtles manage to navigate back and forth.

A green turtle swimming in the waters of the Cayman Islands is marked with a living tag (a piece of white plastron grafted into the carapace) showing that it was released from the Cayman Turtle Farm. Unfortunately, poachers killed this turtle a few months after the picture was taken, before it could reach reproductive age.

Celestial navigation is generally rejected on the basis that sea turtles' eyes are too near-sighted out of the water to be able to distinguish star patterns. Furthermore, sea turtles are able to maintain straight courses even on overcast nights. They might, however, be able to use the direction of the rising and setting sun and moon to calibrate a course based on wave direction. The suggestion that sea turtles follow dissolved odor trails was challenged on two grounds. First, satellite tracking indicates that migrating turtles take very straight and direct courses, while they would more likely follow zig-zag paths to detect odor gradients. Second, scientists have demonstrated that, along some migratory paths, the prevailing currents flow in the wrong direction to carry an odor trail to the feeding grounds. Although it is possible that the sense of smell plays a role in guiding the turtle to a specific nesting area once it is close to its destination, it cannot explain the precise navigation across vast areas of open ocean.

Scientists have found small amounts of magnetite, a naturally occurring magnetic mineral, in the heads of adult sea turtles. It is likely that magnetite functions in some way as part of an internal biological compass. Hatchling turtles have shown the ability to detect two characteristics of the earth's magnetic field that could enable them to place themselves on a magnetic map of the earth. It is very likely that adults retain this ability, and that they use their magnetic sense during their breeding migrations. However, when scientists attached powerful magnets to the heads and shells of turtles nesting at Ascension Island and tracked them by satellite back to the coast of Brazil, the tracks of the magnetically disturbed turtles were virtually identical to those of unmolested turtles. The researchers concluded that turtles do not require magnetic information to navigate home from Ascension and that the navigational methods used by sea turtles remain a perplexing mystery.

It seems likely that turtles are able to use multiple sources of information to help guide them. The turtles swimming from Ascension Island may have been able to use wave direction to guide them on the first part of their journey, then homed in on low-frequency sounds from breaking waves, and finally upon odors from land run-off as they approached the Brazilian coast. Later experiments in which turtles with transmitters were released at various positions around the island showed that the turtles were able to find their way back to Ascension only from downwind. This

This living tag visible on the carapace of a large green turtle was implanted when the turtle was very small, many years before this photo was taken. An external tag would not have stayed on for so long.

implies that airborne odors or sounds may be used in navigation, even though sea turtles have not been shown to use their sense of smell in air.

The puzzle of how migrating turtles find their way to their feeding and breeding locations is linked to the mystery of how these positions are identified in the first place. For years, biologists suspected that sea turtles return to nest in the same areas where they themselves hatched. This was finally confirmed by tests that showed that mtDNA, which is passed directly from mother to offspring, is unique to each nesting area, and shared among all the females that nest there. For example, hawksbill turtles nesting at seven different locations in the Caribbean were found to have genetic "markers" that were mostly unique to turtles nesting in the individual areas. This would explain why several breeding areas that were wiped out by overexploitation centuries ago were never recolonized, even after complete protection of the nesting beaches. Grand Cayman Island hosted, at one time, the largest breeding colony of green turtles in the Caribbean, if not the world. There are still thousands of green turtles in the Caribbean, so you would think that if the beaches of Grand Cayman were simply the best for laying turtle eggs, green turtles would have started nesting there again, but very few have done so.

The loyalty to the beach of origin is strong, but not absolute. If turtles did not wander, new nesting

Green sea turtles crowd a pen at the Cayman Turtle Farm in the British West Indies. These adults are the breeding stock. They lay their eggs on the artificial beach in the background.

A Kemp's ridley sea turtle returns to the ocean after nesting at Rancho Nuevo, Mexico, the prime nesting beach for this Critically Endangered species. Efforts to establish a second nesting colony by transporting eggs from Mexico to Padre Island, Texas, were abandoned in 1989. In 2002 a record thirty-seven Kemp's ridley nests were found on Texas beaches. The increase in nesting in Texas may be a due to seasonal closure of the shrimp fishery (which killed many females as they approached the nesting beach), maturation of the turtles hatched from the transported eggs, or both.

beaches could never be established, and sea turtle populations would go extinct as geological changes eliminate beaches. During the last ice age, 10,000 years ago, nesting would not have been possible on some of today's most important nesting beaches. Recently turtles have even started nesting on artificially created beaches. The similarity of mtDNA among the females within each nesting colony implies that most of these sites were probably established by a single, or only a few, egg-bearing females. Leatherback turtles tend to wander between nesting beaches more than other sea turtles.

Since turtles from each nesting colony have a unique genetic code, could this code include the instructions for the location of the nesting beach, instinctively programming each member of the population to return to that beach to breed? Genetic studies indicate that current breeding populations have probably not been separate for a long enough time to fix an absolute homing instinct into the genetic code.

Imprinting—a process by which important recognition information is fixed into an animal's memory early in life—might explain how turtles recognize their natal beach. Imprinted characteristics could include the position of the beach on a magnetic map, the smell of the beach sand or sea water, or the sound pattern of waves breaking on that beach, and so forth. Experiments have shown that hatchling sea turtles are able to recognize, by smell, sea water from the beach on which they hatched, and that they prefer it to sea water from other sources. Scientists have also shown that hatchlings can use magnetic information to navigate from the natal beach out to sea. It is possible that various sorts of information regarding the natal beach can be imprinted and stored in the turtle's memory until it is time to breed—a span of up to a half century or longer.

If imprinting provided the entire solution to the mystery of natal homing, then it should be an easy matter to re-establish nesting colonies in places where they have been destroyed and even to establish new ones in areas where they never existed, merely by transporting eggs or hatchlings to the desired location. In fact, several such projects have been undertaken. During "Operation Green Turtle" from 1959 to 1968, more than 130,000 green turtle hatchlings and eggs from Costa Rica were distributed to seventeen countries in the Caribbean region. Some of those turtles should have already reached sexual maturity, but the hatchlings were not marked, so no one knows if any survived to breed. Due to a lack of knowledge about proper handling of eggs and hatchlings at the time, survival rates may have been low.

Another experiment is underway at Grand Cayman, where turtles and eggs from several different areas were brought to the Cayman Turtle Farm to establish a captive breeding population. Since 1980, more than 30,000 surplus hatchling and yearling green turtles have been released in Cayman waters. Farm personnel have marked some of these young turtles with "living tags" (shell implants that grow with the turtle) so they can be recognized if they come back to breed. Will these turtles return to Cayman to breed, or perhaps find their way to their ancestral breeding grounds? There may be an answer soon.

Researchers have also attempted to use imprinting to establish an alternate breeding area for the Kemp's ridley turtle. Nearly all of the breeding females of this highly endangered species nest on a single stretch of beach on the northeastern coast of Mexico. Historically, however, one or two females have nested at Padre Island, Texas, each year. From 1978 to 1992, researchers attempted to establish a second breeding colony on Padre Island using eggs from Mexico. They allowed the eggs to hatch in Padre Island sand, "headstarted" the hatchlings for six to nine months in a nearby facility, returned them briefly to the beach at Padre Island for additional imprinting, then released them at sea. The research team marked many of these hatchlings with living tags.

From 1996 through 2002, beachgoers spotted thirteen marked turtles from the headstart program nesting along the Texas coast. This number does not represent a significant increase over the normal amount that nest there, however. Kemp's turtles that nested in Florida and the Carolinas may have also come from the headstart experiment. Some researchers have speculated that the turtles might not have been properly imprinted, and are now "disoriented," wandering about looking for places to nest. One headstarted turtle nested once in Texas and then laid a second clutch in the same season at the main nesting beach in Mexico. It was suggested that the turtle might have followed other migrating turtles to the main nesting beach. It could be that a turtle locates its natal beach through a combination of imprinted information, genetic information, and socially obtained information. The subject of imprinting remains a mystery. If it does occur, we still do not know how, or what types of information are involved.

As these green sea turtles mate in the waters off Malaysia, the female swims the couple toward the surface to breathe. A sharksucker (remora) clings to her plastron.

As these olive ridley turtles mate off a nesting beach in Costa Rica, the male uses his flipper claws to grasp the female. Olive ridleys are unusual among sea turtles in that they are frequently seen mating in open ocean. They more often mate close to nesting beaches, where most sea turtle mating occurs.

The habits of females have dominated the discussion about breeding migrations thus far, but what about males? Recent genetic research shows that males also breed within their birth colonies, but they do so less faithfully than females. Before the nesting season, males also migrate to the place where they hatched, in order to mate. Males, however, are more likely than females to take advantage of opportunities to mate along the way, spreading some of their genes into other breeding populations. This difference is most likely due to the fact that females are only sexually active for one to two weeks, compared to one to two months for males. Olive ridleys, and probably leatherbacks, sometimes mate far out to sea, at great distances from any nesting beaches, possibly providing greater opportunity for genetic mixing among the populations of these two species. Male turtles do not have the burden of producing several loads of eggs during a breeding season, so they may be able to make breeding migrations more often than females. Perhaps some migrate every year. This would increase the ratio of males at the breeding ground, intensifying competition, and ensuring that the strongest, fittest males fertilize the eggs.

The incredible journey to the breeding area is followed by an equally precise return to the feeding area, meaning that the exact location of each turtle's feeding range is also somehow imprinted in its brain. The late Archie Carr collected stories from turtle boat captains of turtles that had been captured, branded, and sent off to market, only to escape during storms. Some of the turtles were later recaptured at the exact rocks where they had previously been taken, often hundreds of miles from the escape point. More recently, scientists who use tags and satellite transmitters to track turtles have documented the same phenomenon. The amazing navigational abilities of sea turtles are now well-established, but researchers have yet to discover exactly how they work.

CHAPTER 7

Troubled Times

ABOVE: These olive ridley eggs are ready to be bagged for sale.

LEFT: This green turtle in Hawaii suffers from numerous FP tumors. While turtles along some parts of the Hawaiian coast do not have FP tumors, close to 100 percent of turtles in other areas are infected. High amounts of runoff from shore and high levels of nutrients in the water are linked to the occurrence of FP. The large amount of algae that covers this reef is a good indication of high nutrient levels in the area.

Until human beings dominated the planet, sea turtles occupied warm seas in prodigious numbers around the globe. Sea turtles were so prominent that they may have exerted some degree of control over tropical marine ecosystems, such as seagrass beds and coral reefs. Sea turtles have survived many global upheavals, including the ice ages and the great catastrophe that wiped out the dinosaurs 65 million years ago.

After the appearance of humans more than one million years ago, sea turtles' ancestral predisposition to lay their eggs onshore put them in great peril. Within the past 1,000 years, human populations, which were small and isolated at first, have grown exponentially, placing any edible creature with such vulnerable females and young in a precarious position. Until 500 years ago, exploitation of turtle meat and eggs was limited by what local populations could consume. As cash economies and international commerce expanded, however, so did the market for turtle products. International trade meant that turtles could be captured almost anywhere in the world and shipped to distant markets where demand always exceeded supply. By the end of the eighteenth century, some major nesting colonies were entirely wiped out.

With the growth of human populations, more sea turtle populations around the world suffered heavy exploitation, more local breeding populations were extirpated, and entire species began to face the threat of extinction. Because some sea turtles do not breed until they are half a century old, recovery from any population decrease is very slow. Under such circumstances, even slight increases above natural death rates can cause populations to continue to decline.

As the environmental awareness movement began to take hold during the last part of the twentieth century, governments issued laws to protect sea turtles. Consumers began to refuse to buy sea turtle meat or eggs, or products made from sea turtles, such as tortoiseshell combs and cosmetics containing turtle oil. Some sea turtle populations have started to recover under protection, but most are still decreasing. One

A green sea turtle and other bycatch lie on the deck of a shrimp trawler off the coast of Costa Rica. In this area, as in many others, TEDs are required by law, but their use is rarely enforced, leading to many unnecessary sea turtle deaths. Photo © Randall Arauz / Seapics.com.

Tar patches soil the main nesting beach for Kemp's ridley sea turtles at Rancho Nuevo, Mexico. Natural oil seeps and artificial sources, such as oil spills and bilge-pumping by ships, can all cause tar patches to form. Even small amounts of tar can kill hatchlings, should they eat it, while a major oil spill could wipe out an entire year's nesting effort. In 1979, in the world's largest known oil spill disaster, the blowout of the oil well Ixtoc I released an estimated 140 million gallons of crude oil into the Gulf of Mexico. The oil slick narrowly missed the Rancho Nuevo beach shortly after the nesting season, and may well have killed an unknown number of hatchling and posthatchling turtles.

A hawksbill rises toward the surface in the pristine waters of Layang Layang Atoll, in the Spratly Islands. For now, sea turtles are relatively safe in this remote oasis of marine life, but their future is clouded by political disputes and the threat of military action, oil prospecting, and long-range fishing fleets.

species, the Kemp's ridley, has been yanked back from the very brink of extinction.

As we progress into the twenty-first century, direct exploitation continues to threaten many populations of turtles, but is no longer a menace to others. However, even sea turtle populations that are presently stable or increasing are jeopardized by a whole range of threats, including pollution, destruction of habitat, incidental capture in fisheries, and diseases promoted by human-induced changes in the environment.

How many sea turtles existed before the onset of intense human exploitation? We have no reliable information on which to base a solid estimate. We can be certain, however, that prior to the arrival of Columbus, the Caribbean was home to many times more than the tens of thousands of green turtles that inhabit the area today. Controversial ecologist Jeremy Jackson has estimated that anywhere from 36 to 660 million green turtles once lived there. If so, such large numbers of grazing animals would have had a profound effect on seagrass beds and other marine habitats, just as the great herds of wildebeest and other herbivores control the environment of east Africa.

The largest green turtle rookery in the Caribbean at the time was on the islands that Columbus named the "Tortugas" or "Turtle Islands," called the Cayman Islands today. Jackson estimates that 6.5 million turtles nested there at the time. He quotes one of Columbus's men as reporting that "the sea was thick with them . . . so numerous that it seemed that the ships would run aground on them, and were as if bathing in them." British settlers from Jamaica colonized the desolate and uninhabited Caymans primarily to exploit the nesting turtles. A century and a half after Columbus arrived, British settlers still described the number of nesting turtles as "infinite." At that time, 13,000 female turtles per year were being hauled away as they came up onto Cayman's beaches to lay their eggs. The harvest continued for another century, but after the last breeding female was taken, Cayman turtlers moved on to exploit other populations. By the end of the twentieth century, fewer than ten green turtles per year nested in the Caymans.

Hawksbill turtles in the Caribbean are also a fraction of their former numbers. Jackson proposes that they once numbered in the tens of millions and may have been a major factor in controlling the abundance of sponges (the principal item in their diet) on these reefs.

Hawksbills have been hunted primarily for their beautiful carapace scutes, the source of "tortoise shell" used in jewelry and decorative items. Green turtles are taken mainly for their flesh, fat, and plastron cartilage ("calipee"), the main ingredient in green turtle soup. Green and olive ridley turtles have been harvested for their skin, which is used to fashion leather goods. Leatherbacks have been killed for their oil. All sea turtles are hunted for their meat, even the hawksbill, which is sometimes poisonous, and the leatherback, which many consider unpalatable.

The beauty of the hawksbill's carapace scutes has been the turtle's undoing. Millions of hawksbills have been killed for their shells alone.

A display of confiscated products made from endangered species includes a tortoiseshell fan, comb, case, and broach.

Humans have heavily exploited the eggs of all species of sea turtles, consuming them as food, health elixirs, supposed aphrodisiacs, and as an ingredient in baked goods. Harvesting the eggs can eliminate a population of turtles, even without taking any adults. Because of the very long life spans of sea turtles, and the length of time it takes them to mature, it may appear as if no damage is done, even as the population is being destroyed. For a turtle that takes thirty years to mature and has a reproductive life of thirty years, for example, females could continue to nest for sixty years after people start taking 100 percent of the eggs. Eventually the population crashes hard, and is not able to rebound.

An olive ridley continues to lay its eggs at Ostional Beach in Costa Rica, even as villagers collect eggs from nearby nests in a controlled, legal harvest. The local residents are allowed to collect eggs only from a certain section of the beach, and only during the first thirty-six hours of an arribada. The arribadas typically last about five days, so it is likely that many of the eggs laid during the first couple of days would be unearthed by other turtles anyway.

This was the case in Terengannu, Malaysia, which once had the world's second largest leatherback rookery. A legal, "managed" egg harvest allowed poachers to sell nearly all of the eggs. The government deemed that this practice had no effect on the population. The few remaining eggs were placed in a hatchery where the temperature of incubation may have produced all females. More than one-third of the eggs were infertile, possibly due to a shortage of males. Trawl and drift-net fisheries also killed adults unintentionally. The number of nesting females declined from more than 1,600 in 1956 to two to four between 1998 and 2000, with local extinction predicted for 2003. A large olive ridley rookery was decimated in the same place by the same methods.

As industrialized fisheries have expanded over the past few decades, incidental sea turtle mortality has rivaled intentional harvest of sea turtles and their eggs as a cause of the decline in sea turtle populations. Among the most deadly types of gear are shrimp trawls, in which usually less than 10 percent of the catch is shrimp. Sea turtles caught in shrimp nets often drown before the net is brought to the surface. Shrimp trawls were apparently the major factor driving Kemp's ridley turtles toward extinction before area closures and TED requirements greatly reduced the death toll.

A TED, or "turtle excluder device," consists of a trap door that ejects turtles while retaining most of the shrimp. If large enough, TEDs are highly effective at reducing turtle deaths. However, in some countries they are still not required, and in many places shrimpers refuse to use them, or they sew them shut so that the devices do not function. In Orissa, India, a trawling ban has not been enforced, and trawlers have been operating right in front of one of the world's most important nesting beaches for olive ridley turtles. A local environmental group estimated that 75,000 ridleys were killed by fishing activity in Orissa during a five-year period.

Other types of indiscriminate fishing gear, such as drift nets and longlines, can be equally devastating to sea turtle populations. A rapidly expanding Chilean swordfish fishery, using gill nets and longlines, was blamed for the collapse of the eastern Pacific stock of leatherback sea turtles. At the most important nesting beach on the Pacific coast of Mexico, the number of leatherback nests declined from 4,800 during the 1986 to 1987 nesting season to 624 in the 2000 to 2001 season. During the 2001 to 2002 season, researchers counted less than half as many leatherback nests in

LEFT: Villagers wash and bag turtle eggs collected during the legal, controlled harvest at Playa Ostional. By giving the local residents an economic stake in the mass nesting of turtles near their homes, managers believe they have encouraged them to remove beach debris that would impede nesting; report poachers; and take other actions to protect the nesting population of turtles. The program remains controversial.

BELOW LEFT: A boy in Indonesia washes green turtle eggs to prepare them for market. Photo © Franco Banfi / Seapics.com.

BELOW: Bags of olive ridley sea turtle eggs from Ostional Beach are legally offered for sale alongside fruit and vegetables at the municipal market in San Jose, Costa Rica.

TOP: A green sea turtle is trapped in a turtle net in the Cayman Islands. Even though turtles are raised for food at the Cayman Turtle Farm and wild populations have not begun to recover from the complete destruction of the world's largest green turtle rookery there, islanders with a permit are allowed to harvest wild sea turtles because it is considered part of their cultural heritage.

RIGHT: This juvenile olive ridley turtle lost one flipper after it became entangled in a nylon rice bag. The vast amounts of floating artificial debris now covering the world's oceans pose an enormous and growing threat to the well-being of sea turtles and other marine creatures. Photo © Robert L. Pitman / Seapics.com.

all of Mexico as on the single beach the year before. A similar rapid decline occurred at the other major nesting beach in Costa Rica. Researchers have concluded that the entire eastern Pacific leatherback population is headed for extinction.

Fishing gear does not have to be in use to kill sea turtles. Every year more and more turtles are killed when they become entangled in abandoned fishing gear. Yet this is only a small part of the rapidly growing problem of marine debris. Plastic items in particular can float around the ocean for years killing sea turtles both by entanglement and by ingestion. Plastic bags and other indigestible items can become impacted in the turtle's digestive system, causing the turtles to starve to death. Leatherback and juvenile loggerhead turtles seem programmed to swallow any floating object within reach. A plastic bag's resemblance to a sea jelly probably adds to the problem. A study of posthatchling loggerheads off the coast of Florida found that 32 percent had plastic in the stomach. Floating tar balls, from natural oil seeps, oil spills, and bilge pumping by ships, also pose a hazard and are becoming more common as shipping increases. The Florida study found that 63 percent of the posthatchling loggerheads had tar in the mouth, stomach, or both. Tar balls, plastics, and other floating debris collect at convergence zones where currents meet—right where sea turtles come to feed. Oil spills themselves can be deadly to turtles at sea and to hatchlings on contaminated beaches.

In 2001, more than 100 turtles were found dead after a chemical factory located near an important nesting beach in the Mediterranean released chromium waste. Such events grab headlines, but a much more insidious threat is the daily runoff of sewage, fertilizer, and other substances into the water surrounding nearly all human settlements. This wastewater carries nutrients that promote the growth of algae, which can kill corals and seagrasses, damaging both the habitat and food sources of sea turtles.

High nutrient levels can also promote the growth of dinoflagellates, the group of microscopic organisms that includes the microbes responsible for red tides and the flesh-eating "cell from Hell" that attacks fish and humans. At least one type of dinoflagellate produces a chemical that appears to promote the growth of fibropapilloma (FP) tumors. Green turtles have been the hardest hit by the recent plague of fibropapilloma (FP) tumors, possibly because this dinoflagellate lives on types of algae that green turtles like to eat. FP tu-mors are grotesque, warty masses that grow on both the inside and outside of sea turtles, killing the turtle slowly, often by interfering with its ability to feed.

Discovered in 1936, FP has only become common in recent years. In some areas, as many as 100 percent of sea turtles are afflicted with it. There is a strong correlation between the prevalence of the disease and sources of pollution from shore. The dinoflagellate does not cause the disease. A herpes virus, similar to the types that infect humans, is believed to be the actual infectious agent. A chemical produced by the dinoflagellate, however, appears to make the turtle much more likely to develop tumors if infected.

FP has now been found in every ocean basin in the world, and in every species of sea turtle. FP has

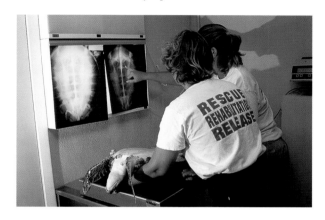

At the Turtle Hospital in Marathon, Florida, Sue Schaf and Corinne Rose examine x-rays of a green turtle suffering from FP tumors. FP tumors can be surgically removed, often leaving the turtles tumor-free for years afterwards. This is, however, one of very few facilities in the world able to perform this service.

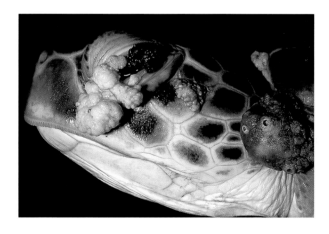

FP tumors, which often start on or near the eyes, block the vision of this green sea turtle in Florida.

RIGHT: A portion of this female olive ridley turtle's carapace has been crushed, probably by a collision with a boat. She is nesting on a Costa Rican beach.

ABOVE LEFT: A biologist uses a microwave scanner to read a P.I.T. (Passive Integrated Transponder) tag implanted in the flipper of a Kemp's ridley turtle nesting at Rancho Nuevo, Mexico. The rice-grain-sized P.I.T. tags are retained better than traditional external metal flipper tags, which often tear loose and become lost.

ABOVE RIGHT: A volunteer places cloth mesh over a wire cage surrounding a Kemp's ridley nest inside the nest "corral" at Rancho Nuevo, Mexico. The cloth prevents the entry of flies, which lay their eggs in the nest, producing maggots that attack the turtle eggs. The wire cage and corral fence keep out larger predators.

become a global pandemic that poses a serious threat to a number of populations, but it is not the only disease that kills sea turtles. In late 2000, loggerhead turtles in Florida suddenly began floating to the surface, afflicted with some unknown malady that left them paralyzed. Nearly 200 loggerheads became stranded during the epidemic, which lasted into 2001, and most of them died. Throughout the world's oceans, epidemics of new or formerly rare diseases are becoming more prevalent among various groups of organisms, as human activities alter the environment and the slow accumulation of chemical pollutants weakens the organisms' immune systems.

Global warming is likely to affect sea turtles in numerous ways. Aside from more rapid proliferation of disease organisms, sea turtles will lose nesting beaches as sea level rises and will lose habitat, as coral reefs die due to higher water temperatures. Higher nest temperatures will alter the sex ratio in hatchlings, and eventually beach temperatures may reach lethal levels.

Sea turtles are already rapidly losing nesting habitat to humans. Development of nesting beaches can prevent turtles from nesting there or reduce their success. Lights and other disturbances may discourage females from nesting on the beach. Dogs and other animals introduced by humans may destroy the nests. Artificial lights often lure hatchlings away from the ocean to die in the hot sun or be run over by cars. Sea walls and other "protective" structures can accelerate erosion and block access to suitable nesting sites. "Beach enhancement," the dumping of dredged sand to widen eroded beaches, sometimes produces beaches with sand so compact that the turtles cannot dig nests. In some places, motorboats frequently strike turtles as they surface to breathe. Turtles can also be injured and killed by the concussion of explosives detonated for fishing, military purposes, oil platform removal, or oil exploration.

Around the world, people are pitching in to try to save sea turtles. Volunteers walk nesting beaches, moving nests to safe locations and guarding them until the eggs hatch. Special hospitals treat turtles with tumors and injuries from boats and fishing gear. Concerned citizens have mounted public information campaigns to discourage people from consuming turtles and their eggs.

National laws, such as the U.S. Endangered Species Act, and international treaties, such as the Convention on Migratory Species, have been highly effective in protecting some populations of sea turtles. The

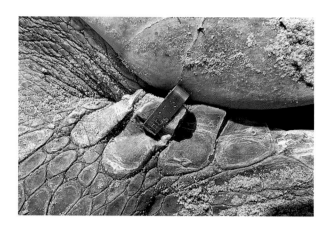

A metal identification tag is attached to the flipper of a Kemp's ridley turtle nesting at Rancho Nuevo, Mexico. The tag will enable researchers to compile a nesting history of this individual when she returns to nest again, or may help determine migration routes if the turtle is captured or strands elsewhere.

Convention on International Trade in Endangered Species (CITES) has been instrumental in eliminating the international markets for turtle products which often drive exploitation.

Nonetheless, sea turtles remain in dire straits. Status designations vary from country to country, and sometimes between different parts of the same country. The International Union for the Conservation of Nature and Natural Resources (IUCN) 2002 Red List, however, classified sea turtles worldwide as follows: Leatherback, hawksbill, and Kemp's ridley turtles—Critically Endangered; loggerhead, olive ridley, and green turtle—Endangered; Mediterranean subpopulation of green turtle—Critically Endangered; flatback turtle—Data Deficient.

To avoid driving sea turtles into extinction, we must continue and expand the campaigns to protect sea turtles from direct exploitation and indirect killing as fisheries bycatch; protect nesting areas; reduce the amounts of pollutants and debris entering the ocean; and educate the public on the needs of sea turtles. But these measures will be insufficient if human populations continue to climb steeply. Specific conservation actions can reduce some types of human impact and prolong the survival of many species, but as our numbers continue to grow, so will our cumulative impact. The direct and indirect effects of human activities make the environment less and less hospitable to most other species, dooming sea turtles and other vulnerable animals not capable of adapting to rapid change.

CHAPTER 8

Families and Species

ABOVE: The elongated prefrontal scales, distinctive to the green sea turtle, are clearly visible above the nostrils and between the eyes of this juvenile specimen. Most sea turtles have two pairs of shorter prefrontals. Only the green turtle and flatback have a single pair, while the leatherback has no scales (except as a hatchling). The pattern created by the scales on the green turtle's face is unique to each individual, and can be used to identify specific turtles during studies.

LEFT: Scuba divers commonly see three sea turtle species—the loggerhead, the hawksbill, and the green turtle, shown here. When trying to differentiate among these species, divers can look at the head, carapace scutes, and coloring of the turtles. The loggerhead turtle has a larger, more block-shaped head than the green, while the head of the hawksbill is more slender with a pointier beak. On the green turtle, the carapace scutes abut each other, while on the hawksbill they overlap. The loggerhead is more reddish-brown in color than the other two species.

Green Sea Turtle, *Chelonia mydas* (family Cheloniidae), "So Excellent a Fishe"

Of the seven species of sea turtles, the green turtle is the one that most people think of when sea turtles are mentioned. Also known as the "edible turtle," it is the one most highly prized for food. The green turtle was so well regarded in Bermuda that by 1620 the legislature saw the need to pass an act protecting "so excellent a fishe." (The legislation did not prevent the complete extirpation of the Bermuda green turtle rookery, however). The flesh is considered savory, but the most esteemed part of the green turtle is the calipee—a cartilaginous substance that is scraped from the inside of the plastron and used as the main ingredient in green turtle soup. The body fat can be rendered for oil, which has been used for cooking, cosmetics, medicines, and numerous other products. The greenish color of the fat is believed to be the origin of the turtle's name.

These two green sea turtles have been resting on the bottom at a cleaning station in Hawaii, and are about to head to the surface for a breath of air. Because green turtles reside for years in very limited areas, they are likely get to know each other and have regular interactions (such as competition for the best resting spots and for the attention of cleaner fish). Scientists have yet to complete any studies on the social structure (if any) of turtle communities, however.

The shell and skin vary in color, including shades of green, brown, black, white, gray, and yellow. The carapace scutes of juveniles often feature rayed patterns, and can be just as beautiful as those of the hawksbill. But they are rarely fashioned into jewelry or decorative items because they are much thinner than hawksbill scutes, and not as easily worked. The upper body and shell tend to be dark, while the underside is white to yellow to pale orange.

The green turtle grows to the second largest size of any sea turtle, with a maximum shell length of 55 inches (140 cm) and a maximum weight of 517 pounds (235 kg), but most individuals are considerably smaller. When compared to other sea turtles, with the exception of the hawksbill, the green turtle's head is small in relation to its body. The pattern of scales on the head is highly distinctive; most other sea turtles have two pairs of squarish-to-pentagonal prefrontal scales, while the green turtle has only a single elongated pair. The green turtle is also the only species with tooth-like serrations on the lower jaw. The carapace has four lateral scutes (compared to five on the loggerhead) and a smooth margin (compared to the jagged margin on all but the largest hawksbills).

Range

The green turtle occurs in tropical to subtropical waters worldwide, and breeds in scattered locations throughout the warmer parts of that range. Breeding populations were probably more evenly distributed at one time, but many were likely extirpated due to human activities. Various regional populations are genetically distinct, often exhibiting slight differences in appearance and body measurements. The Mediterranean green turtle and Hawaiian green turtle, for example, form distinct populations. Of these populations, the eastern Pacific green turtle, or black turtle, which breeds along the west coast of Mexico, Central and South America, and in the Galápagos Islands, is the most unique in appearance. Some authorities accord the black turtle species status, as *Chelonia agasizzi*. The black turtle is smaller, darker, and has a slightly steeper and narrower carapace than the green turtle. An analysis of body measurements suggested it could be a separate species. Studies of skull shape and genetics, however, indicated that the black turtle is at best a subspecies of *Chelonia mydas*. The issue is a source of fierce debates, in which conservation politics play a major role.

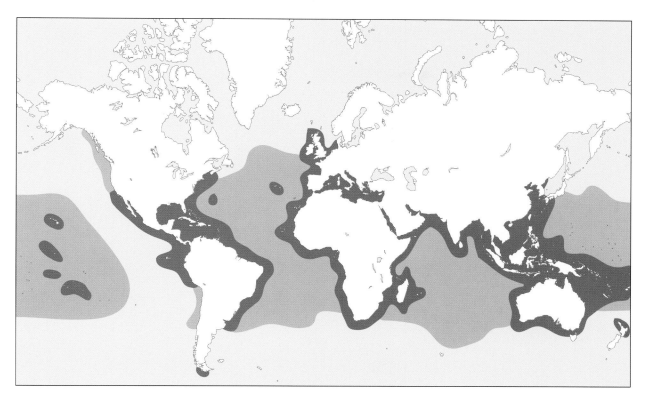

ABOVE: Green sea turtle

■ High-frequency sightings

■ Low-frequency sightings

LEFT: A green turtle rises toward its reflection on the surface of shallow waters around Grand Cayman Island. This turtle is likely one that was released as a yearling from the Cayman Turtle Farm. In the next few years, researchers should begin to find out how such turtles fare reproductively.

A green turtle feeds on green algae in the northern Galápagos Islands. Green turtles, like most other animals, cannot digest the cellulose in plant material on their own. Green turtles, like cows and termites, process cellulose only with the help of symbiotic bacteria. In green turtles, bacterial fermentation occurs in the large intestine. All other sea turtles eat primarily animal material.

Development

Hatchlings swim out to sea from the nesting beach, and spend two to ten years or longer in the pelagic environment. When they reach a shell length of between 8 and 17 inches (21–44 cm), they move inshore, and adopt a bottom-dwelling lifestyle.

Benthic juvenile greens may share habitat with adult turtles, but they can also be found in developmental habitats where adults are rare or absent. After leaving the pelagic habitat, green turtles stay mostly in shallow water, where there is enough sunlight for plants to grow. Feeding grounds usually contain a mixture of turtles from various breeding beaches. Some may originate from breeding beaches close to the feeding area, but usually most come from distant areas. The life span of the green turtle is unknown, but is believed to be similar to that of humans.

Diet

During the pelagic phase, juvenile green turtles are believed to subsist largely on a diet of sea jellies and other soft-bodied invertebrates that float in surface waters. After leaving the pelagic environment, they undergo a radical dietary shift, becoming the only sea turtle that is primarily vegetarian. As in rabbits and horses, bacterial fermentation in the turtle's hindgut is essential for the digestion of plant matter.

The actual diet varies by location and what is available, but green turtles seem to prefer seagrasses. When they crop seagrass, they stimulate the growth of new shoots, which are more nutritious than the older blades. By continually re-cropping their "pastures," the turtles condition the seagrass beds to be more productive, possibly exerting a strong influence on the ecology of seagrass habitats. Where seagrasses are not abundant, green turtles feed mostly on various types of algae, showing strong preferences for certain types. In coastal estuaries, they also feed on the leaves, shoots, and roots of mangrove trees. On occasion, green turtles may also consume a small amount of animal matter. Juveniles in particular continue to take sea jellies when available. Benthic phase green turtles consume more sponges than any other type of animal matter. Most of these are probably taken in unintentionally with grass or algae. Molluscs, worms, small crustaceans, soft corals, tunicates (sea squirts), and small fish (probably scavenged) have also been found in the stomachs of green turtles.

Due to their low-protein diet, wild green turtles grow more slowly than other sea turtles. In captivity, where green turtles can be easily conditioned to accept high-protein fish or pelletted food, they grow much faster.

Some populations and individual green turtles feed chiefly at night, especially in areas where they have been heavily exploited. After sixteen years of protection under the Endangered Species Act, juvenile and subadult green turtles in some areas of Hawaii reverted from nighttime feeding to daytime feeding.

Reproduction

Captive green turtles can reach sexual maturity in as little as eight years, but in the wild, green sea turtles grow much more slowly and at a highly variable rate, depending on their diet. Recent estimates suggest that most wild green turtles mature at twenty to sixty years of age. The average age at which maturity is attained varies from place to place, and is estimated at twenty-six to thirty-four years old in Florida and forty years or older in Australia.

At the onset of maturity, both males and females start to make regular breeding migrations back to their beach of origin. Some of these migrations involve open ocean voyages of thousands of miles. Green turtles that feed along the coast of Brazil, for example, swim halfway across the Atlantic to breeding beaches on the small island of Ascension. Without any landmarks, green turtles must navigate with precision over a distance of 1,400 miles (2,300 km) to reach this landfall. Female greens typically make the breeding migration every two to four years, although the actual interval can vary from one to nine years for different individuals. Males migrate at more frequent intervals, typically one to three years.

Most mating occurs close to the nesting beach, although some occurs at more distant locations, possibly during the migration. Mating has been observed for as long as six hours in the wild and five days in captivity. Both sexes are promiscuous, and eggs within a single clutch may be fertilized with sperm from one to four different males. In general, females only mate during a brief receptive period, usually about four weeks before they lay their first clutch of the season. Females lay from one to nine clutches (average about three) at intervals of about one to two weeks. The number of eggs in a clutch can vary from one to 230. The average clutch size varies by location, but is usually about 112. Green turtles in some areas sometimes deposit some small yolkless eggs in the nest along with the fertile eggs, but this is much less common than in leatherback turtles. The eggs incubate for an average of about forty-seven to seventy days (depending on location and season).

Basking

Green turtles are the only sea turtles known to come ashore for purposes other than nesting. Both immature and adult males and females are known to "bask" in the Galápagos and Hawaiian Islands. Occasional basking has also been reported in Australia and Mexico. Green turtles bask both by day and by night. Basking may serve multiple purposes. Basking might allow egg-bearing females to escape the attentions of amorous males and to raise their body temperature, which speeds up egg maturation. It may also serve, for any turtle, to reduce the risk of shark attack and to allow the turtle to conserve energy as it waits for favorable tides for feeding. When basking occurs by day, it could also accelerate digestion, increase synthesis of

A pair of mating green sea turtles is pursued by two males attempting to join the action. Green turtle mating is often a rowdy affair, with up to eight males competing for a single female.

A late-nesting green turtle is still covering its nest as dawn breaks at the Turtle Islands Park in Sabah, Malaysia. The park, which straddles the boundary between Malaysia and the Philippines, is one of the world's first transnational conservation areas.

vitamin D, and promote healthy skin by weakening or killing external parasites, algal growths, and bacterial or fungal infections.

Dormancy

Fishermen off Baja, Mexico, in the Gulf of California, and off Florida in the Gulf of Mexico, have reported that green turtles bury themselves in the mud during cold weather. In both areas, the fishermen believed that the turtles over-wintered in the mud in a state of hibernation.

Unfortunately, this behavior made it very easy for divers to capture the dormant turtles. The Seri Indians had apparently captured dormant turtles in Mexico for subsistence purposes for centuries. But after commercial markets developed, both the Baja and Florida green turtle populations were quickly overexploited. By the time scientists heard about this strange phenomenon in the 1970s, they were unable to find any turtles to study in order to determine if they really hibernate for long periods or if they just bury themselves temporarily, and come up to breathe after a few hours.

Farming

The green turtle is the only species of sea turtle that is commercially farmed. The Cayman Turtle Farm in the British West Indies raises thousands of green turtles for local consumption and as a tourist attraction. The farm also releases small turtles into local waters in an attempt to replenish the depleted local population. The farm is owned by the Cayman Islands government, which purchased it when the previous owners were unable to make a profit after the CITES agreement banned international trade in sea turtle products.

Conservation Status

Green sea turtles in the wild continue to be threatened by direct harvest of turtles and eggs, incidental take in other fisheries, degradation of nesting beaches and feeding habitat, pollution, climate change, and disease. However, protective legislation and conservation initiatives have reversed downward trends in several populations, notably the ones that nest in Florida, Hawaii, Tortuguero (in Costa Rica), and the Turtle Islands in Malaysia. The number of nests produced by these populations has shown an upward trend during

This juvenile green turtle at a research facility has a living tag. Researchers create these tags when turtles are still hatchlings by exchanging a plug from the turtle's carapace with one from the plastron. For all of the turtles hatched in a particular year, researchers implant the white plastron plugs into the same part of the carapace. Plugs are placed in a different part of the carapace each year so that the turtles' ages can be determined when they are sighted later. Implanted wire tags are the only other type of tags that can be applied to hatchlings and retained until the turtle is an adult, but these tags cannot be seen from the outside.

the past thirty years. The Tortuguero nesting colony is by far the largest in the Atlantic/Caribbean region, so the trend is especially encouraging. However, some scientists caution that the current population in the Caribbean may still be as little as 1 percent of the numbers during prehistoric times. A troubling development worldwide is the rapid increase and spread of fibropapilloma disease. The FP pandemic may reverse the progress that has been made in restoring some populations.

Worldwide, the green turtle is listed as Endangered by the IUCN, except for the Mediterranean subpopulation, which is listed as Critically Endangered. In the United States, under the Endangered Species Act, the green turtle is listed as threatened, except for the Florida subpopulation, which is listed as Endangered. In Australia, it is listed as Vulnerable.

Loggerhead Turtle,
Caretta caretta (family Cheloniidae), "Big Red"

The orange-brown color of the loggerhead sea turtle's carapace and upper body scales makes it easy to identify. The underside and exposed skin vary from white to yellow to pale orange in adults. Juveniles are darker. The oversized, blockish head, which has two pairs of prefrontal scales, is also a distinctive feature. The somewhat spindle-shaped carapace (compared to the rounder carapaces of most other sea turtles) has five pairs of lateral scutes. Barnacles and other external growths are more common and varied on loggerheads than on any other type of sea turtle. The loggerhead is the third largest sea turtle (after the leatherback and green), with a carapace length of up to 49 inches (124 cm) and a weight of up to 398 pounds (181 kg).

Range
Loggerheads are found worldwide in tropical to warm temperate areas and are the only sea turtles that nest extensively in the temperate zone. The two largest nesting areas are at Masirah Island, Oman, in the Arabian Sea, and along the southeastern coast of the United States. They are more common along continental margins than around oceanic islands, and have been found as far north as Newfoundland, and as far south as Argentina. Juveniles especially may feed in temperate areas seasonally and migrate to warmer zones in winter. In subtropical areas, loggerheads may move to warmer waters offshore during the winter, or bury themselves in sediments and enter a torpid state.

Development
After hatching, loggerheads spend a developmental period in open ocean. The length of the pelagic juvenile phase varies greatly. In the Atlantic it is estimated to last three to fifteen years. In the Pacific, fifteen years is considered a minimum. During this time they are likely to travel completely across the ocean and back at least once, and may swim long distances seeking out rich feeding areas along the edges of strong currents and at boundaries between cool, plankton-rich waters and warm, clear waters. One tagged loggerhead swam more than 5,600 miles (9,000 km) in fifteen months. Loggerheads hatched in Japan cross the Pacific to feed on pelagic crabs off Baja California, Mexico, traveling roughly one-third of the way around the earth. This is one of the longest migrations known in marine animals.

Loggerheads generally begin to leave the pelagic habitat and appear in shallow water when they reach a shell length of 16 to 25 inches (40–64 cm) in the western Atlantic, and 28 to 31 inches (70–80 cm) in Australia. They occupy a variety of shallow water habitats, including soft-bottom lagoons, hard-bottom limestone banks, coral reefs, and seagrass beds. When not foraging, they usually find a cave, crevice, coral head, or shipwreck in which to rest. Loggerheads that reach adulthood are likely to live for decades under natural conditions, with some individuals living to an age of sixty or older.

The loggerhead is the sea turtle species that divers in Florida and the Bahamas are most likely to see. Whereas the scutes of most hawksbills overlap, the carapace scutes of adult loggerheads join evenly, like those of the green turtle. Like the hawksbill, the loggerhead has four prefrontal scales behind the nostrils and between the eyes, whereas the green has two longer prefrontal scales in the same location.

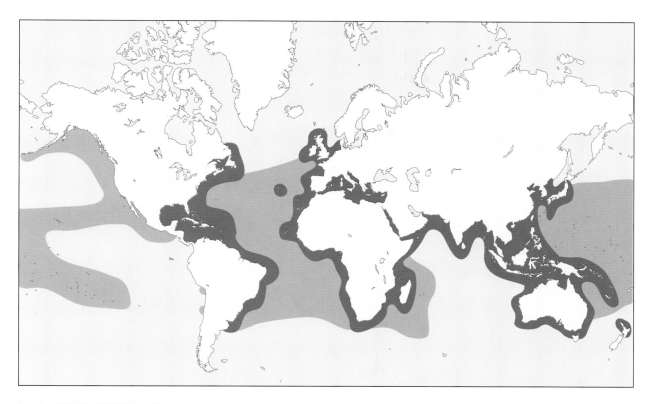

ABOVE: Loggerhead sea turtle
■   High-frequency sightings
▨   Low-frequency sightings

LEFT: Gooseneck barnacles nearly cover the carapace of a pelagic juvenile loggerhead. Loggerheads seem more prone than other sea turtles to encrustations of various organisms.

BELOW LEFT: A pelagic juvenile loggerhead off the Azores Islands is accompanied by a small fish, which uses the turtle as a mobile reef. This overhead view shows the five lateral scutes, which distinguish the loggerhead from the green and hawksbill, both of which only have four lateral scutes on the carapace.

A loggerhead turtle in the Bahamas feeds on a triton shell. The large head and heavy beak of the loggerhead are well adapted for its diet of shellfish.

Diet

The loggerhead's massive head contains powerful jaw muscles, used to crush the shellfish that form the basis of the adult turtle's diet. Loggerheads have a broader diet than most other sea turtles, showing a preference for crustaceans and molluscs, including crabs, lobsters, barnacles, conchs and other sea snails, and scallops; but also feeding on other benthic invertebrates, such as worms, sea urchins, sea biscuits, soft corals, and sea cucumbers. They sometimes destroy traps to reach the lobsters or crabs inside, and will scavenge fish discarded from trawlers or other sources. Loggerheads specialize in locally abundant food sources in some areas, such as Chesapeake Bay, where they feed on horseshoe crabs. In the Gulf of Mexico, they feed heavily on crabs when abundant and switch to sea pens (a type of soft coral) when crabs are not available. Posthatchlings, juveniles, and some adults feed in surface waters of the open ocean, consuming pelagic snails, crabs, shrimp, and worms; fish eggs; sea jellies and similar organisms; barnacles that grow on floating objects; sargassum weed; insects; dead fish and squid; debris; and almost anything else that floats by.

Reproduction

The age of sexual maturity is highly variable among individuals and among ocean basins. Scientists believe that some individuals might begin to breed at age twenty, and others might not reproduce for the first time until they are sixty years or even older. It is believed that most loggerheads do not start to breed until they are twenty to thirty years or older in the Atlantic, and at least thirty-five in the Pacific. They are estimated to continue to breed for about thirty-two years on average.

Females make breeding migrations at intervals of one to seven years (averaging two to three). During a breeding season they produce one to seven clutches of eggs at intervals of about two weeks. Each clutch contains an average of 110 eggs. The eggs incubate for an average of fifty to sixty-nine days, depending on location.

Dormancy

Loggerhead turtles, like green turtles, sometimes bury themselves under bottom sediments during winter months. Loggerheads that were dredged up from a channel at Cape Canaveral, Florida, appeared to be in a torpid state and were covered with mud. The author once saw a loggerhead buried in sediments off West Palm Beach, Florida. As with green turtles, there has been some speculation that loggerheads might hibernate in the mud for weeks or months. However, some researchers believe that the turtles stay in a dormant state for no more than a few hours before surfacing to breathe. No studies to date have been able to determine how long the turtles stay buried.

Conservation Status

Worldwide, loggerheads are listed as Endangered by the IUCN. In the United States they are listed as Threatened. In eastern Australia, where the loggerhead population is estimated to have declined by as much as 90 percent since the 1960s, they are considered highly endangered. Although they are not greatly esteemed for their flesh in most areas, the eggs are highly valued for baking and as supposed aphrodisiacs. In eastern Australia, foxes prey heavily upon the eggs and in other parts of the world other animals pose a threat. Fishermen hunt loggerheads in some places, but many more are killed accidentally in fisheries. Loggerheads are highly vulnerable to capture by trawl nets, longlines, gill nets, and drift nets. In the Azores Islands of Portugal, more than 4,000 juvenile loggerheads from the southeastern United States population are captured each year on longlines set for swordfish. Another 20,000 are taken by longlines in the Mediterranean, and more by longlines and gill nets off North America. In the Pacific, at least another 4,000 juvenile loggerheads are taken in pelagic fisheries each year. In Australia and South Africa, loggerheads and other sea turtles are also killed by nets and hooks set to reduce shark populations near swimming beaches.

Because of their tendency to try to eat anything they see, loggerheads, especially posthatchlings and juveniles, are particularly likely to ingest tar, plastics, and other dangerous substances. The author once saw a pelagic juvenile eating a floating plastic bucket, bite by bite.

As with other species, development and degrada-

A loggerhead turtle drops eggs into its nest on Juno Beach, Florida. The southern Florida population of loggerheads is the second largest breeding population in the world (after Oman). These turtles are genetically distinct from the population that breeds from northern Florida through Georgia and the Carolinas, and from the population that breeds in the Florida Panhandle.

tion of nesting beaches is a problem, particularly in Florida, where artificial lighting and beach armoring affect large areas of nesting habitat. Boat strikes and diseases are among the other causes of mortality. In 2001–2002, nearly 200 loggerheads washed up in Florida dead or paralyzed from a previously unknown disease, possibly associated with a biotoxin or parasitic flukes that attack the nervous system.

Hawksbill Turtle, *Eretmochelys imbricata* (family Cheloniidae), "The Glass-Eater"

The hawksbill is one of the three sea turtles most likely to be seen by divers and snorkelers, as it typically inhabits coral reefs (with some individuals occurring on rocky points, in lagoons, and in seagrass or algae beds). The hawksbill, reaching a maximum carapace length of 45 inches (114 cm) and a maximum weight of 189 pounds (86 kg), does not grow as large as the leatherback, the green turtle, or the loggerhead. The hawksbill's small head and pointy, bird-like beak make it easy to identify. Hawksbills are also usually distinguished by a jagged rear margin on the carapace, defined by the sharp points of the scutes. Whereas the carapace scutes of other sea turtles fit together like a mosaic, the hawksbill's scutes are imbricated, with each scute overlapping the one behind it (except in very old individuals). These scutes, known as carey or bekko, are the raw material from which tortoiseshell items are produced. There are four pairs of lateral scutes on the carapace (compared to five pairs on the loggerhead), and two pairs of prefrontal scales on the head (compared to one pair on the green). The carapace scutes have beautiful rayed patterns in various shades of brown, black, clear, and gold, while the plastron is cream-colored.

Range

Hawksbills occur throughout the tropics, and breed only in the tropics. Of all sea turtles, the hawksbill is the least likely to stray into temperate regions. Unless they have been hunted, hawksbills will be found wherever coral reefs occur. Hawksbills, however, are not social, so large aggregations do not occur.

Development

It appears as if in some areas, after hawksbill hatchlings crawl out of the nest and down to the ocean, they do not go into the sustained swimming frenzy that green, loggerhead, and leatherback turtles do. Some individu-

A hawksbill turtle swims over a coral reef at Layang Layang Atoll. Although this photograph does not clearly show the pointed beak or imbricated scute pattern typical of the hawksbill, the presence of two claws on each foreflipper allow for a positive identification. (The only other sea turtle with two flipper claws is the loggerhead, and it does not occur in this locale.)

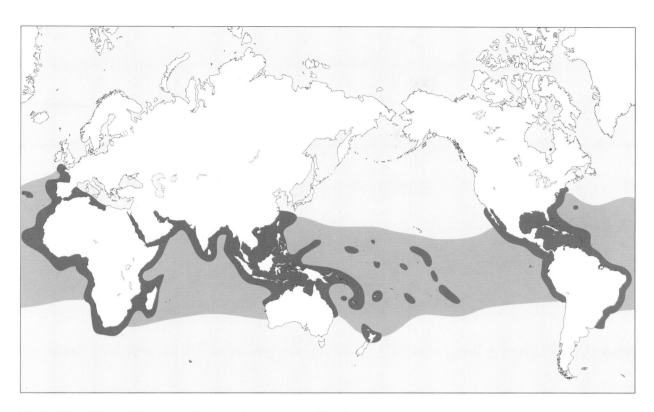

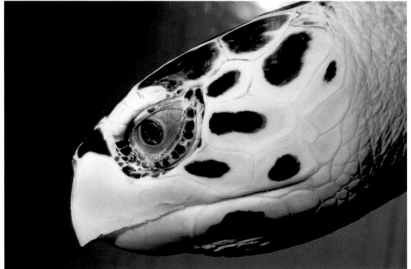

ABOVE: Hawksbill sea turtle
High-frequency sightings
Low-frequency sightings

LEFT: The bird-like beak of the hawksbill is evident in this photo taken at a public aquarium.

This hawksbill turtle, photographed in Grand Cayman, has lost some of the scutes at the rear of its carapace. Nonetheless, the jagged rear carapace margin typical of young hawksbills is plainly visible.

als may swim vigorously for a few hours, and others hardly at all. Those that do not swim away may just skip the pelagic developmental migration, and grow up close to home. This may be essential to maintaining populations around isolated island groups such as Hawaii and the Seychelles. Genetic tests indicate that most turtles hatched in the Seychelles spend their whole lives there. Hawksbills smaller than 8 to 14 inches (20–35 cm) are rarely seen on reefs, however, so it is not known where turtles that might skip the pelagic stage could be hiding. Some hatchlings, on the other hand, may drift and swim for several years, ending up far from home. In the Caribbean, some hawksbills settle close to their natal beaches while others establish residence far away and must later migrate back to breed. The turtles feeding in any given area may come from a number of breeding beaches within a range of hundreds of miles in the Caribbean, or up to 1,500 miles (2,400 km) in the Pacific.

Once they have settled onto a reef, hawksbills establish a feeding territory. They may occupy the same feeding territory throughout their lives, or they may move to new territories as they mature. One large immature hawksbill crossed the Atlantic Ocean from Brazil to Senegal, traveling at least 2,300 miles (3,680 km) in six months. Most establish an adult territory within a few hundred miles of their natal beach. Adults often feed on deeper reefs than juveniles, diving to at least 330 feet (100 m). When one hawksbill encounters another within its territory, a squabble often ensues. Generally one turtle then leaves the immediate area, and neither is injured. The longevity of hawksbills is unknown, but is probably considerable, given that scientists estimate that decades pass between the time they settle on the reef and when they start to reproduce.

Diet

Although very little is known about posthatchling hawksbills in the open ocean habitat, it appears that they eat mostly the same foods as pelagic-phase turtles of other species, including sea jellies and other jelly-like creatures, pelagic snails, fish eggs, pelagic crabs, and other floating organisms. After settling to the bottom, hawksbills retain their omnivorous habits, but generally concentrate on sponges. One study in the Caribbean found that 95 percent of the hawksbills' diet consisted of sponges. Very few other animals eat sponges because sponges employ chemical and physical defenses to make themselves unpalatable. Most

A female hawksbill covers her nest in Malaysia, close to the equator. Hawksbills live and breed almost exclusively in the tropics.

sponges are loaded with toxic and noxious compounds, and their bodies are usually reinforced with either tough fibers, sharp slivers of limestone, or needles of glass-like silica. Interestingly, hawksbills seem to prefer the silica-containing sponges to the fibrous ones. This has prompted researchers to refer to them as having a "diet of glass." Hawksbills have been known to eat sponges that are deadly both to fish and to other turtles. Humans have died from eating hawksbills, probably due to retention of the sponge toxins in the turtle's flesh.

In the Indian and Pacific Oceans, sponges are not nearly as prominent on reefs as they are in the Caribbean. Hawksbills in these areas often feed on cryptic sponges, which grow on the underside of dead coral. They often overturn coral rubble while looking for food, and sometimes even demolish branching coral skeletons. Only close observation reveals that the turtles are actually consuming sponges. The retinue of sponge-eating fish that sometimes gathers around them provides another clue that sponges are the target. Angelfish often follow feeding hawksbills to feed upon the sponges that the turtles have broken open. Angelfish avoid the outer layers of sponges, which apparently contain a substance that deters even fishes that can eat the inner sponge tissues.

Other items found in the digestive tracts of hawksbills include sea squirts, anemones, crabs, snails, sea urchins, squid (undoubtedly scavenged dead), barnacles, corals, hydroids, bryozoans, algae, seagrass, stones, plastic, wood, bark, seeds, and leaves. There is some question as to whether hawksbills can digest plant matter, and they certainly cannot digest stones and plastic, so it is likely that they consume some items by mistake or as mechanical aids to digestion.

Reproduction

Estimates of when hawksbills reach sexual maturity run from ten to twenty-two years or older in the Caribbean to thirty years or older in the Seychelles and Australia. Hawksbills nest mostly by night, but in a few locations they nest primarily in the late afternoon. In general hawksbills have a less defined nesting season than other sea turtles. In a few places, nesting is

A hawksbill hatchling prepares to enter the sea. Unlike other sea turtles, which may swim hard for more than a day to get far from shore, some hawksbill hatchlings may swim for only two hours, then settle someplace close to their natal beach. Other hawksbills may swim as far as 1,500 miles (2,400 km) from the beaches where they hatched.

concentrated on certain beaches, but throughout much of their range, hawksbills tend to nest alone in scattered locations. Some scientists, however, argue that this pattern is a result of centuries of over-exploitation, which left behind only remnants of what were once large nesting colonies.

Like other sea turtles, hawksbills usually nest near where they hatched themselves. The nesting beach may be a short or long swim from their feeding area. Some turtles that feed in Australia, for example, nest in the Solomon Islands. Although females usually return to nest every two to three years, some nest every year, while others wait ten years or more before nesting again.

During a nesting season, a hawksbill lays one to seven clutches at intervals of about two to three weeks. The number of eggs in a clutch averages 130. Incubation lasts an average of forty-seven to seventy-five days, depending on location and season.

Conservation Status

In spite of the risk of poisoning, humans consume hawksbills throughout most of the tropics. Hawksbill eggs are eaten throughout the turtle's range, and in some areas poachers take nearly 100 percent of the eggs laid. The market for tortoiseshell is the primary cause for the decimation of hawksbill populations, however. The tortoiseshell trade dates back at least to the reign of Queen Hatsheput of Egypt in the fifteenth century B.C. Tortoiseshell, which has been traded worldwide for millennia, was highly valued by the ancient Romans, Chinese, and Arabs, at times achieving the value of gold and ivory. More recently, Japan has purchased the bulk of traded tortoiseshell, importing the scutes of more than one million hawksbill turtles between 1970 and 1986.

The tortoiseshell trade and egg harvesting have been disastrous to hawksbill populations all over the globe. At one time, Chiriqui Beach in Panama was the major nesting beach in the Caribbean, hosting as many as 900 nesting hawksbills per night in the 1950s. In a 1980 survey, researchers counted only seventeen nesting tracks. By 1981 that number had dropped to thirteen, and by 1990 only one nest was found. It is likely that many populations were greatly depleted or completely extirpated before scientists ever began to make surveys.

The international trade in hawksbill products fell sharply when Japan stopped importing tortoiseshell in 1994, but illegal commerce continues, mostly in

A hawksbill gnaws on a coral head at Layang Layang Atoll. Close examination will reveal that the turtle is scraping encrusting sponges from dead portions of the coral

Asia. Japan has recently proposed to reopen its hawksbill markets, prompting some fishermen to continue hunting turtles and storing the shells as an investment for the future. And people still hunt hawksbills for local use, including ceremonial feasts in Indonesia. Egg poaching continues on a large scale. Small hawksbills are sometimes stuffed and sold as curios to tourists.

Studies of migration and residency patterns have important implications for management. Some fishermen in the Seychelles resisted protection of the declining stocks there, claiming that they would only be caught by fishers in other countries, until research indicated that the local hawksbills do not migrate outside the Seychelles. Conversely, Cuba's proposal to harvest its hawksbills for international trade was discredited when it was shown that turtles in Cuban waters come from populations that nest in other countries as well.

Hawksbills are subject to the variety of threats that affect all sea turtle species, including debris ingestion; oil spills and other forms of pollution; entanglement in fishing gear; boat strikes; destruction and alteration of nesting habitat; climate change; and disease. Because of their dependence on coral reefs, hawksbills may be particularly susceptible to global environmental changes. Coral reefs have declined dramatically in the past few decades, and are continuing to deteriorate at a rapid pace. The causes of the decline are numerous and complex, but warming of ocean waters seems to be responsible for the most widespread coral die-offs.

The number of hawksbills that remain is unknown, but populations continue to decline fairly rapidly in many areas. Notable exceptions are Mona Island in Puerto Rico, Cousin Island in the Seychelles, and the Yucatan Peninsula of Mexico, where hawksbill nesting has actually increased in recent years. In U.S. waters, hawksbills are listed as Endangered and in Australia as Vulnerable. On a global basis, the IUCN lists them as Critically Endangered.

Olive Ridley, *Lepidochelys olivacea* (family Cheloniidae), "The Party Animal"

The olive ridley is the smallest of the sea turtles, reaching a maximum carapace length of 31 inches (78 cm) and a maximum weight of 106 pounds (48 kg). Adults are slightly darker than the similar Kemp's ridley, ranging from gray to brown to olive on top and from yellowish to creamy white on the underside. The carapace is nearly round and slightly higher than the Kemp's ridley. There are two pairs of prefrontal scales on the head. The olive ridley is unique among sea turtles in having a variable number of lateral scutes on the carapace. The number can vary from five to nine (usually six or seven) and a turtle may have more scutes on one side than on the other.

Range

There is little chance of confusion between the two ridley species, as the olive ridley is almost entirely absent from the Kemp's ridley's range and vice versa. The olive ridley occurs throughout the tropical to warm-temperate parts of the Pacific and Indian Oceans and, during periods of unusually warm sea water, has been sighted as far north as Alaska and as far south as New Zealand and Chile. The bulk of the population, however, is found in the tropics. In the Atlantic, the distribution is limited mostly to the western coast of Africa and the northeastern coast of South America, occasionally extending into the West Indies. The olive ridley is not normally found in the Gulf of Mexico and most of the North Atlantic, where the Kemp's ridley is found.

Enormous nesting aggregations occur in India and along the western coasts of Mexico and Costa Rica. Relatively few olive ridleys nest in the Atlantic. The

A male olive ridley turtle looks for action off the coast of Costa Rica. Studies have not yet determined how much gene flow occurs among different breeding populations of olive ridleys due to this species' habit of sometimes mating in blue water far from the nesting beach. Under these circumstances, a male from one population could easily fertilize the eggs of a female from a different breeding location.

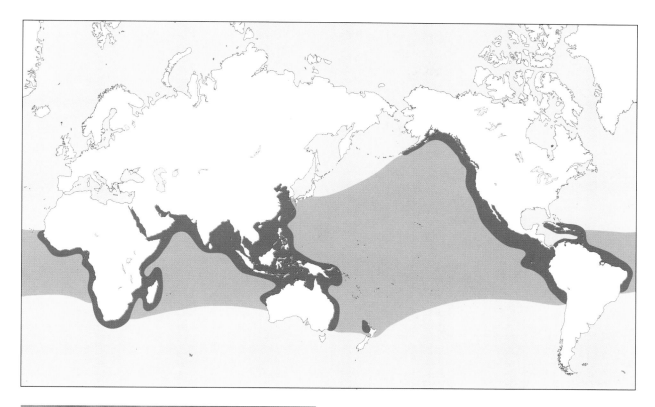

ABOVE: Olive ridley sea turtle
■ High-frequency sightings
▨ Low-frequency sightings

LEFT: An arribada ("arrival") of olive ridley turtles coming ashore to nest at Playa Ostional in Costa Rica. Some authorities prefer the term "arribazon," which is Spanish for "great arrival."

majority of nesting on Atlantic beaches occurs in Surinam, French Guiana, Angola, and Namibia. In spite of its relative scarcity in the Atlantic, the olive ridley is probably the most abundant sea turtle in the world.

Development

Olive ridley hatchlings, like those of other sea turtle species, usually emerge from their nests at night. On beaches where mass nestings have occurred, hundreds of thousands of hatchlings may pour into the sea at once. The hatchlings swim furiously out to sea, but the duration of the swimming frenzy is not known in this species. A few sightings of posthatchlings near flotsam and their overall dark color lead to the presumption that they may hide in drift lines, but scientists know very little about either the posthatchling or the juvenile phase of the olive ridley.

Any attempt to estimate the length of the pelagic developmental stage is complicated by the fact that many large juveniles and adults regularly forage on the high seas, even though most are found in coastal waters. Olive ridleys are apparently able to utilize both coastal and pelagic environments. In pelagic circumstances, olive ridleys stay mostly within the tropics, whereas loggerheads and leatherbacks more often feed in higher latitudes of the open ocean, where the cooler waters are more productive. Olive ridleys are able to

A pair of olive ridley turtles mate off the coast of Costa Rica. Great assemblages of sea turtles reported to stretch for many miles off the Pacific coast of Central America may consist of olive ridleys, migrating toward their breeding beaches.

sustain themselves in tropical pelagic waters by diving deeper to feed where the warm surface water meets the cooler and richer water underneath. Their dives into cooler waters may explain why olive ridleys are the turtles most likely to be seen basking at the surface, with their shells dried by the sun.

Olive ridleys apparently grow rapidly and mature quickly compared to most other sea turtles. Early maturation implies a shorter life span, but the longevity of the olive ridley is not known.

Diet

In the pelagic environment, olive ridleys prey on sea jellies and jelly-like organisms, including the venomous Portuguese man-of-war, comb jellies, and drifting relatives of sea squirts. They also eat pelagic snails, shrimp, and crabs; fish eggs; and dead squid and fish when available. They gnaw gooseneck barnacles, algae, and other organisms off floating objects. In coastal waters, olive ridleys feed on crabs, molluscs and a variety of other invertebrates, and sometimes fish. In one study, large quantities of puffer fish were found in the stomachs of olive ridleys, but the turtles may have scavenged the fish from the discarded bycatch of shrimp boats.

Reproduction

Olive ridleys apparently reach sexual maturity at an early age, probably within the range of seven to sixteen years estimated for the closely related Kemp's ridley sea turtle. Olive ridleys typically mate in front of the nesting beach like most sea turtles, but they also mate in the open ocean. Researchers spotted one pair mating more than 620 miles (1,000 km) from the nearest nesting beach. Olive ridleys nest mostly on the beaches of continents and large islands, and rarely on small oceanic islands. Preferred nesting sites are on relatively flat beaches near the mouths of rivers and estuaries. On a small number of these beaches, arribadas occur. It is a measure of our ignorance of the natural history of sea turtles that olive ridley arribadas were unknown to science as recently as the 1960s.

The scale of arribadas can boggle the imagination. At one site in Costa Rica, there have been estimates of up to 500,000 nests produced in a single five-day arribada. Other species of sea turtles, notably greens, sometimes nest in large concentrations, but only olive and Kemp's ridleys nest in the highly coordinated fashion that defines an arribada. These two species are

As she returns to the sea after nesting, an olive ridley turtle tramples and crushes another turtle's eggs, which have been un-earthed by yet another turtle in the frenetic activity of a mass nesting. The hatching success of eggs laid during arribadas is much less than that of eggs laid by solitary nesting turtles, leading biologists to question the value of this reproductive strategy.

apparently able to hold fully developed eggs "on standby" for up to a month or longer, awaiting the environmental and/or social stimuli that trigger an arribada. Arribadas tend to occur roughly at intervals of one lunar month, but are somewhat variable and unpredictable. Factors associated with the occurrence of arribadas include high winds, tidal state, and lunar phase. The presence or activity of other turtles in the aggregation may also help to trigger the arribada, but the social component remains mysterious. Sometimes the same individuals nest simultaneously and close together on successive arribadas, but they do not appear to associate between arribadas, and migrate separately at the end of the nesting season. Adverse environmental conditions, such as unusually heavy rainfall, can apparently delay an arribada.

The adaptive function of arribadas also remains somewhat mysterious. The most-accepted idea is the "predator satiation hypothesis," which proposes that concentrating reproduction into a small segment of space and time will exceed the consumptive capacity of nearby predators, allowing most of the offspring to

escape once predators have had their fill. Research has confirmed that the chance of an olive ridley nest escaping predation by raccoons, coyotes, coatis, crabs, and snakes is better during an arribada than for solitary nesting. Terrestrial predation on the eggs, however, is probably minor compared to what happens to the hatchlings once they hit the surf. It remains unknown whether it is possible to satiate the appetites of the many predators in the marine environment, including those that may come specifically to take advantage of an abundant food source.

One problem with this strategy is that the nesting density during arribadas is often so high that nesting females dig up and break eggs from earlier nests. Because arribadas occur at monthly intervals and incubation takes nearly two months, baby turtles do not escape the nest before the beach is plowed up again. The broken eggs nourish bacteria, fungi, and insects that can infest undamaged nests. Contamination can reduce hatching success at major arribada beaches to less than 1 percent. Where arribadas occur on long beaches, they may shift between sections of the beach,

An olive ridley hatchling paddles to the surface for a breath while migrating offshore from the nesting beach. The "belly button" scar marks the spot where the yolk sac was attached in the egg.

raising hatching success to more than 30 percent. Where ridleys nest on a solitary basis, however, hatching success can be as high as 80 percent.

Some scientists hypothesize that arribadas may be events that build up and die off at certain beaches over the years, as part of a natural cycle. Solitary nesting occurs all along the coast near arribada beaches. If hatchling survival is high at a certain beach, then more turtles will eventually return to that beach to nest. Over many generations, enough turtles may accumulate at that beach during the nesting season to trigger an arribada. Years of arribadas may contaminate the sand and attract more predators, leading to a decline in hatchling survival, and an eventual reduction in the number of nesting turtles. In time the arribada may dwindle away at that location, even as arribadas are building up at other locations.

Olive ridleys that nest alone generally emerge from the sea at night. During arribadas, most nesting occurs at night, but it can spill over into daylight hours, ceasing only during the hottest part of the day. The small ridleys are able to dissipate heat better than larger turtles, and are usually able to get up the beach, nest, and get back into the water in an hour or less, which is much faster than other turtles. Clutch size varies, averaging around 105 eggs in most locations. The number of nests laid per season is lower than most sea turtles, averaging one and a half, but the olive ridley compensates for this low rate with more frequent nesting migrations. More than half of olive ridleys nest on a yearly basis, with others usually nesting at two- or three-year intervals. Individuals that nest more than once during a season average seventeen days between nestings if they nest alone, and twenty-eight days if nesting in arribadas, which are often synchronized with the lunar cycle. The incubation period averages forty-five to sixty-five days, depending on location and season.

Conservation Status

The olive ridley's ability to adapt to a wide variety of habitats and food sources no doubt contributes to its success in maintaining large populations, at least in the Pacific and Indian Oceans. Rapid growth and early maturity probably also help.

The spectacular arribadas at some breeding locations are encouraging, but obscure the fact that many olive ridley populations are still declining. The IUCN lists olive ridleys as Endangered worldwide. Under the U.S. Endangered Species Act, the Mexican breeding population is listed as Endangered, and all other breeding populations are listed as Threatened. The National Marine Fisheries Service, however, has recommended that the western Atlantic breeding population be reclassified as Endangered. This population has declined more than 80 percent since 1967. In Australia olive ridleys are listed as Endangered.

The causes of the decline in olive ridley populations generally match those for other sea turtle species. The olive ridley is threatened by shrimp trawls and other nets (including those operating illegally off major nesting beaches); longlines; oil spills and other forms of pollution; ingestion of marine debris; development, erosion, and pollution in feeding and nesting areas; artificial lighting on nesting beaches; introduction of nest predators such as dogs and pigs; boat collisions; use of explosives for fishing, construction, oil exploration, or military exercises; climate change; hunting; and egg collection. In Mexico, industrial slaughterhouses were responsible for the collapse of several populations. The slaughterhouses, set up next to the nesting beaches, incorporated processing plants that utilized nearly every part of the turtles, with the most important product being fine leather for luxury goods. Legal controls allowed the survival of some turtles, but populations still declined precipitously until 1990, when Mexico declared total protection for sea turtles. At least one nesting population is making a dramatic recovery, but others may have been completely wiped out.

At Ostional Beach in Costa Rica, a managed legal harvest of eggs takes place during the first thirty-six hours of an arribada, under the theory that these nests would likely be damaged anyway by later-nesting turtles. Although this program is controversial, it is possible that the harvesting actually increases hatching success by reducing contamination of the nesting beach. It has also given local residents a stake in the resource, encouraging protection of the nesting females and environment.

On the Pacific coast of Costa Rica, coyotes have only recently become a threat to olive ridleys. Predation by coyotes was nonexistent in the 1970s and 1980s, but from 1998 through 1999 coyotes destroyed 74 percent of olive ridley nests and killed sixteen nesting females. It is conceivable that such high levels of predation could produce a change from nighttime to daytime nesting in a population of turtles. It is possible that this is exactly what happened in the Kemp's ridley turtle.

Kemp's Ridley, *Lepidochelys kempi* (family Cheloniidae), "The Comeback Kid"

The Kemp's ridley is the rarest, most endangered, and, in many ways, most enigmatic of all sea turtles. For years, biologists were unsure if the Kemp's ridley was in fact a true species. Although the eggs had been harvested for years, the turtle's only nesting location remained unknown to science until 1963. It slid perilously close to extinction before its numbers started to rebound in recent years.

The Kemp's grows to about the same size as the closely related olive ridley, reaching a maximum carapace length of 30 inches (75 cm) and a maximum weight of 108 pounds (49 kg). The ridleys are the two smallest species of sea turtles. The Kemp's ridley is similar in appearance to the olive ridley, with a head that is larger than a green or hawksbill, but smaller than a loggerhead, in proportion to body size. The Kemp's olive-gray-to-brown carapace is slightly lighter in color and flatter than that of the olive ridley. Its plastron is yellowish to creamy white. The Kemp's ridley always has five lateral scutes, while the olive ridley usually has more and the number of scutes can vary. Both species have two pairs of prefrontal scales on the

The light color of this nearly mature Kemp's ridley is fairly typical of adults, while smaller juveniles tend to be darker on top and white underneath. Hatchlings, by contrast, are a uniform olive gray.

head, but there are several major differences in the skulls.

Range

The Kemp's ridley has the most limited distribution of any sea turtle except the Australian flatback. For the most part, breeding is confined to a limited stretch of beach on the Gulf coast of Mexico, with occasional nesting in Texas and Florida. Adults mostly stay within the Gulf of Mexico. Juveniles feed in shallow coastal waters along the Gulf and Atlantic coasts of Mexico and the United States, at least as far north as Massachusetts, but must migrate south in winter or risk death from cold water. Juveniles also have been collected in the open North Atlantic and off the coasts of Europe and North Africa, but it is not known if these are "waifs," destined to be lost to the population, or if, like loggerheads, they are able to find their way back to the western side of the Atlantic.

Distribution maps of the two ridley species are like reverse images, with the Kemp's ridley occurring in exactly the area where the olive ridley is absent. Genetic and other information indicates that the two species diverged from a common ancestor 3 to 4 million years ago, about the time that the Isthmus of Panama divided the Atlantic and Pacific Oceans. One theory holds that the Kemp's ridley evolved into a separate species in the Atlantic, and that the olive ridley only recently entered the Atlantic from the Indian Ocean by swimming around the tip of South Africa.

Development

Hatchlings emerge from the nest mostly between midnight and dawn, crawl to the ocean, and swim out to sea. Hatchlings held for hours before release appear less active than green or loggerhead hatchlings, indicating the possibility of a shorter swim frenzy. This is consistent with the theory that most Kemp's hatchlings stay within the Gulf of Mexico. The Gulf of Mexico provides an ideal nursery area for hatchling Kemp's ridley turtles, with floating patches of sargassum weed in which to hide not far offshore. There is some indication that the hatching season may correspond with the occurrence of seasonal currents that tend to retain the hatchlings within the Gulf. Some of the young turtles, however, are swept out of the Gulf, into the Atlantic, up the eastern coast of the United States, and even across to the eastern North Atlantic. Juvenile Kemp's ridleys tagged as far north

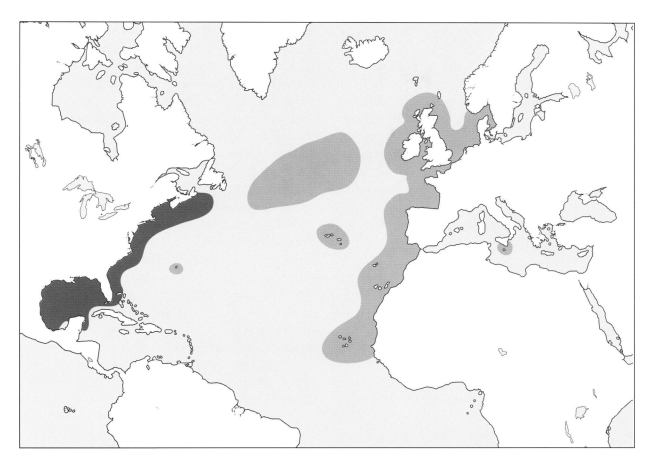

ABOVE: Kemp's ridley sea turtle

■ High-frequency sightings
■ Low-frequency sightings

LEFT: A Kemp's ridley sea turtle lifts its head to breathe. Unlike the closely related olive ridley turtle, Kemp's ridleys do not bask at the surface, but quickly dive again after filling their lungs.

as Chesapeake Bay have later turned up nesting at Rancho Nuevo, but there is no evidence so far of Kemp's turtles returning from the eastern Atlantic.

The pelagic developmental stage is estimated to usually last one to four years. At a size of about 8 to 12 inches (20–30 cm) shell length, juvenile Kemp's ridleys settle to the bottom, moving into shallow, turbid coastal waters to feed. Juveniles entering the bottom-dwelling phase tend to occupy shallower environments than adults and occur seasonally much farther north than adults, which stay mostly in the Gulf of Mexico. The longevity of Kemp's ridley turtles is unknown.

Diet

Kemp's ridley posthatchlings, like those of other sea turtle species, are believed to feed on sea jellies, pelagic snails, and other floating organisms. Unlike the olive ridley, which is a generalized feeder, benthic-phase Kemp's ridleys specialize in crabs, which are especially abundant in the Gulf of Mexico and in East Coast feeding grounds used by juveniles, such as Chesapeake Bay. Kemp's ridleys also consume shrimp and molluscs, and occasionally other invertebrates, such as sea urchins and sea jellies. They feed primarily by day.

Reproduction

Kemp's ridleys are estimated to reach sexual maturity between seven and sixteen years of age. Some mature

A Kemp's ridley turtle nests at Rancho Nuevo, Mexico. The Kemp's ridley is the only sea turtle that nests primarily by day, and the only species that concentrates nearly its entire nesting activity at a single location.

males may stay near the breeding beach all year long, while most females migrate between the breeding beach and preferred feeding areas to the north and south. Kemp's ridleys are the only sea turtles that nest more often by day than by night. It is possible that their ancestors nested at night and shifted to nesting during the day to reduce predation on eggs and females by coyotes, a nocturnal animal that is the primary nest predator for the Kemp's ridley. Coyotes are common along the beaches on Mexico's Gulf coast, where Kemp's ridleys nest. The small size of ridley turtles enables them to disperse heat more efficiently than larger turtles, and allows them to get up the beach, nest, and get back into the water faster than larger turtles. Otherwise, daytime nesting would result in lethal overheating.

As with the olive ridley, some female Kemp's ridleys nest individually, but many participate in arribadas. Solitary nestings often occur during the night and pre-dawn, as well as by day, but arribadas always peak during the day. As with olive ridleys, arribadas tend to occur at roughly four-week intervals, but vary with environmental conditions and are most strongly correlated with high winds. Wind may reduce heat stress and protect against predators by obscuring tracks and nesting odors. The nesting season lasts from April through July, in contrast to olive ridleys, which nest year-round with seasonal peaks.

Females lay an average of two and a half clutches per season, depositing an average of 104 eggs in each clutch. They return to nest again at intervals of one to four (most often two) years. Like olive ridleys, they complete nesting in less than an hour and pound sand over the nest by rocking back and forth. The eggs incubate for forty-five to fifty-eight days, depending on the temperature and humidity.

Kemp's ridleys nest almost exclusively in the area from Campeche, Mexico, north to Padre Island, Texas, with major arribadas occurring only on a small stretch of this beach near the small town of Rancho Nuevo. It has been suggested that nesting may have been more widespread prior to human colonization of the Americas. Archaeological evidence to support this is lacking, but the increase in nesting outside of Rancho Nuevo over the past two decades (since the population has been recovering) supports this idea.

Conservation Status

Scientists were aware of Kemp's ridley turtles prior to 1963, but were baffled by the lack of any indication

An estimated 2,000 Kemp's ridley sea turtles nest in a 1968 arribada. This is much smaller than the 1947 arribada estimated at 42,000 females, but larger than any arribada that has occurred since. Arribadas ceased to occur when the population reached its lowest level in 1985, with only 740 nests being laid during the entire season. By the year 2001, turtles were laying up to several hundred nests per day. Photo by A. Montoya, courtesy of Dr. Rene Marquez.

that they ever reproduced, leading to the supposition that they might be sterile hybrids between loggerhead and green turtles. In that year, a film surfaced that had been taken in 1947 by an engineer and pilot, Andres Herrera, who had landed his plane on the beach at Rancho Nuevo during an arribada. According to Archie Carr's description of the film, published in *The Sea Turtle—So Excellent a Fishe*, "You could have run a whole mile down the beach on the backs of turtles and never have set foot on the sand." Carr pronounced it "the movie of all time . . . the incredible crowning culmination of the ridley mystery."

The number of turtles nesting at Rancho Nuevo on that single day was estimated at 42,000. However, nearly every egg that was laid on the beach was collected, a situation that had apparently been going on for some years. It was not until 1966, when a camp was established to protect and study the turtles, that egg collection finally declined. To protect nests from poachers and predators, they were relocated to a fenced "corral" in front of the camp. The rate of egg poaching was gradually reduced to close to zero. At the same time, however, an increase in shrimp trawling was killing more and more adults and subadults throughout their range. The population continued to plummet, reaching a low of 740 nests for the entire year in 1985. The trend toward extinction was reversed through a combination of continued egg protection, required use of TEDs, and closed areas and seasons for shrimping. The number of nests began a sharp upward trend around 1994, reaching 6,436 in the year 2002.

To reduce the vulnerability of the population to an oil spill or other disaster affecting the single nesting beach, scientists made an attempt to establish a second breeding colony at Padre Island, Texas. From 1978 to 1988, researchers took eggs to Padre Island for hatching and imprinting. The hatchlings were then "headstarted" by rearing them for six to twelve months in tanks in a facility in Galveston, Texas. When the juvenile turtles were judged large enough to have a good chance of survival in the wild, they were taken out in a boat and released into the Gulf of Mexico. From 1989 to 1992, no more eggs were sent to Padre Island, but headstarting continued in Galveston, using hatchlings from Rancho Nuevo. From 1979 to 1993, more than 22,000 headstarted turtles were released, and three-fourths of these were well-marked, but from 1996 to 2002, beach patrols documented only thirteen headstarted turtles nesting on the Texas coast, although it is likely there were some that were missed.

While the current recovery is encouraging, the total population of Kemp's ridley turtles is still small and vulnerable to interactions with fisheries and the large oil extraction industry in the Gulf of Mexico. In 1979 a major oil spill that reached Rancho Nuevo just after the nesting season may have been devastating to posthatchlings at sea. In late 2002 the U.S. government approved a plan to drill natural gas wells in the Padre Island National Seashore. The plan allows heavy trucks to drive across turtle nesting beaches during the nesting and hatching seasons. Development, introduction of predatory animals, and light pollution are concerns around the nesting beaches. As with other species, ingestion of floating debris, climate change, accumulation of heavy metals, PCBs and other pollutants, and disease are all threats. The Kemp's ridley is listed as Endangered under the U.S. Endangered Species Act, and as Critically Endangered in the IUCN 2002 Red List.

A Kemp's ridley hatchling bobs to the surface for a breath, offshore from the nesting beach. This hatchling may spend its entire life in the Gulf of Mexico, or it may travel up the East Coast as far as New York. If it gets caught that far north when cold weather arrives, however, it will die.

Australian Flatback Turtle, *Natator depressus* (family Cheloniidae), "The Homebody"

Oddly enough, the sea turtle that seems to be doing the best job of holding its own in today's turbulent world is the one species that skips the pelagic dispersal phase—a trait that in the past enabled other sea turtles to prosper by colonizing suitable habitats throughout the world. The Australian flatback turtle is one of the most unusual and least known of all the sea turtles.

The flatback was once thought to be a sister species of the green turtle, but is now placed in a separate genus. Its evolutionary relationships with other sea turtles are uncertain. It is a medium-sized sea turtle, reaching a maximum carapace length of 41 inches (103 cm) and weight of 213 pounds (97 kg). The upperside of adults is olive-gray to brownish-gray, with yellowish coloring around the neck, face, and edges of the carapace and flippers. The flatback's underside is creamy white. The turtle's most distinctive characteristic is the upturned rim of the carapace, which creates a shallow trough in the shell that tends to collect sand when a female buries her nest. The scutes covering the carapace and flippers are waxy and so thin that

An Australian flatback sea turtle returns to the sea after nesting. The upturned rim of the carapace, like the brim of a fedora hat, is a distinctive feature of the flatback.

if the flatback scrapes against a branch or a rock it may draw blood. Like the green turtle, the Australian flatback has four pairs of lateral scutes and only one pair of prefrontal scales, but its prefrontals are not nearly as elongated as in the green. The Australian flatback also has a larger head than the green turtle.

Range

The Australian flatback turtle had the luck to evolve in an area that has remained relatively undisturbed and sparsely inhabited. Due to the lack of a pelagic phase in its life history, the flatback's range is limited to the tropical and subtropical portions of the Australian continental shelf, including the southern coast of the island of New Guinea. Flatbacks have a few nesting beaches on the Australian mainland, but for the most part they nest on islands off the northern and northeastern coasts of Australia.

Development

Flatback hatchlings are larger than those of any other member of their family—second in size only to leatherback hatchlings. Producing fewer, larger young may compensate for the lack of a pelagic stage in this species. The hatchlings appear to stay in the nearshore environment where their large size gives them some advantage against the predators that abound in coastal waters. On their way from the nest to the water, their large size gives them near total protection from crabs and gulls on the beach. The hatchlings are apparently buoyant and spend a period of time living at the surface like other sea turtles, but may graduate to a bottom-dwelling existence at an earlier age than other turtles.

During all life stages, flatbacks apparently occupy approximately the same areas, seeming to prefer turbid soft-bottom inshore habitats and avoiding waters deeper than about 130 feet (40 m). When not feeding, flatbacks sometimes bask at the surface. The longevity of flatbacks is unknown, but one female survived at least twenty-two years after her first nesting, which would suggest that the life span is at least forty years.

Diet

Little is known about the food preferences of flatbacks, but they appear to feed on a wide variety of benthic invertebrates. They are one of the few animals known to prey on sea cucumbers, and may even specialize in

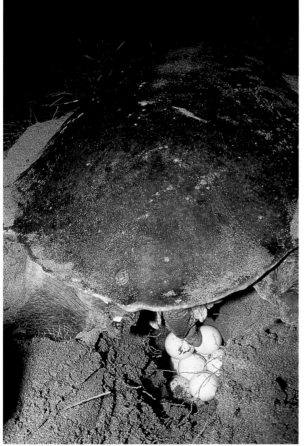

ABOVE: *Australian flatback sea turtle*
■ *High-frequency sightings*
▪ *Low-frequency sightings*

LEFT: A flatback lays her eggs on an Australian beach. The flatback lays eggs that are larger than those of any other sea turtle, except for the leatherback, but lays only about half as many eggs in a clutch as other sea turtles. This female has a data logger attached to the left rear margin of her carapace. This device will record the depth and time of her dives between nestings. When she returns to nest again, researchers will remove the device and download the data to a computer.

An Australian flatback turtle covers her nest high in the beach dunes of an island off the coast of Queensland. Flatbacks are prone to wander well into the dunes while looking for a nesting spot.

this abundant resource. Recorded stomach contents include prawns, sea jellies, squid and other molluscs, hydroids, soft corals, sea cucumbers, algae, and bryozoans.

Reproduction

The few scientists studying Australian flatbacks have not yet obtained sufficient data to estimate the age at which sexual maturity is reached. However, one tagged flatback was first recorded nesting at an age of about twenty years. After reaching maturity, flatbacks migrate between their preferred feeding areas and nesting areas, sometimes swimming as far as 800 miles (1,300 km). Like other sea turtles, they return faithfully to the same nesting area each breeding season.

Flatbacks nest mainly at night, but about 1 percent nest by day. Females lay one to four clutches of eggs per season and return to nest at intervals of one to five years. The clutch size is the smallest of any sea turtle, with an average of fifty-four eggs. This is only about half as many eggs as most sea turtles, but the eggs are much larger—nearly as large as those of the enormous leatherback turtle. The incubation period averages fifty-three days.

Conservation Status

Although Aboriginal people in northern Australia sometimes hunt (legally) flatbacks, many people do not like the flavor of this turtle's meat, possibly due to noxious substances the turtles may acquire from prey such as sea cucumbers or bryozoans. Aboriginal people take flatback eggs more often than turtles. In some areas, animals introduced by humans, including pigs, foxes, and rats, destroy large numbers of nests. Natural predators, including dingos, monitor lizards, night herons, storks, and crocodiles, can also consume significant numbers of eggs and/or hatchlings. At sea, ospreys, pelicans, and sea eagles prey on hatchlings and

A flatback turtle returns to the sea after nesting. She carries a load of sand that was trapped by her upturned carapace brim as she flung sand to cover her nest. In spite of the obvious differences between flatbacks and green turtles, the two species were confused for many years. Even after the flatback was recognized as a separate species, scientists placed the turtle along with the green turtle in the genus Chelonia *until giving it its own genus,* Natator, *in 1988.*

small juveniles, while sharks eat both juvenile and adult flatbacks. Crocodiles sometimes attack adults at nesting beaches in the far north. Some flatbacks are killed by shrimp trawls, shark control nets, and other fishing devices. Flatbacks are also vulnerable to ingestion of floating debris, pollution, climate change, habitat loss, and other environmental ills that affect all sea turtles. Flatbacks are listed as Vulnerable in Australia. An initial listing of Vulnerable in the IUCN 2000 Red List was revised to Data Deficient in the 2002 list to reflect the lack of information about populations of this species.

Leatherback Turtle, *Dermochelys coriacea* (family Dermochelyidae) "The High Seas Cruiser"

Leatherbacks are so different from all other sea turtles that they are classified in a separate family, the Dermochelyidae. The leatherback family diverged from other sea turtles (which belong to the family Cheloniidae) at least as far back as the Cretaceous period (146 to 65 million years ago). The earliest leatherbacks had shells similar to other sea turtles, but over time the bones in the carapace were reduced to a mosaic of tiny pieces only a tenth of an inch (3–4 mm) thick. The bones in the plastron were reduced to a ring around the outside, with only a few bits of bone in the middle, imbedded in fibrous tissue. Instead of scutes, the shell is covered with a layer of oily skin. Small scales protect the bodies of hatchlings, but the adults have naked skin.

Leatherbacks are the largest of all sea turtles, and among the heaviest living reptiles, reaching a carapace length of at least 8.4 feet (256 cm) and a weight of one ton (916 kg). The flippers are longer than other turtles' and can span 9 feet (2.7 m). The bizarre appearance of the long spindle-shaped body is accentuated by the ridges on the shell (seven upper, five lower), the irregular white splotches covering the nearly black body, and the W-shaped upper beak.

Even more remarkable than their appearance are the leatherbacks' physiological adaptations to a lifestyle that is unusual even by sea turtle standards. Leatherbacks are the only sea turtles that feed regularly in cold temperate waters. Observers have even seen leatherbacks surface among pack ice. Leatherbacks are able to survive in frigid waters through a combination of the insulating properties of their oily skin, and

The unusual body of the leatherback turtle, with its soft, ribbed carapace and enormous paddlelike foreflippers, is more exquisitely adapted for long-distance oceanic travel than that of any other sea turtle. Leatherbacks are correspondingly less comfortable in shallow water and on shore than other sea turtles. This female, swimming toward the Pacific coast of Mexico, will probably choose a nesting beach with a short steep slope, where she will have to drag her enormous body the minimum possible distance across the sand to get beyond the high-water mark.

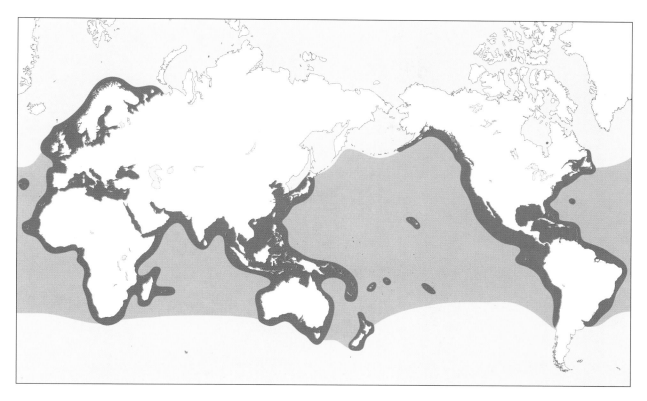

ABOVE: Leatherback sea turtle
■ High-frequency sightings
■ Low-frequency sightings

LEFT: A leatherback turtle hatchling swims in open ocean off the nesting beach. It already shows the oversize foreflippers that also characterize adult leatherbacks. For the next several years, its life will be a mystery. Unlike adult leatherbacks, the hatchling's body is covered with small scales.

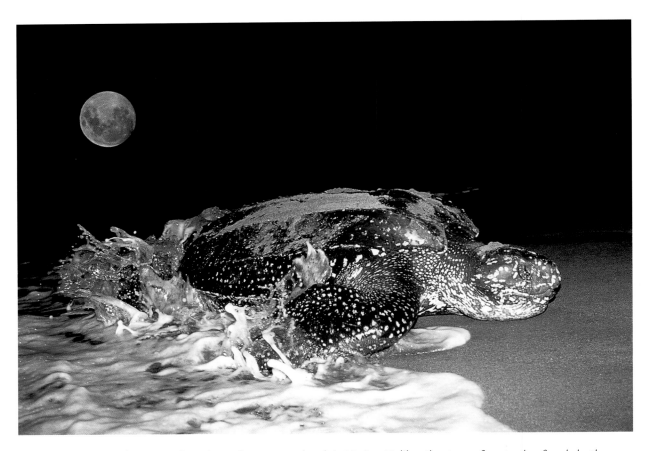

A leatherback sea turtle emerges from the surf to nest on a beach in Mexico. Unlike other types of sea turtles, female leatherbacks in most areas do not face a great risk of being killed by poachers when they come ashore, as the oily meat is generally not highly valued. In some parts of the world, however, poachers may kill nesting leatherbacks only for the meat of the shoulder muscles, which power the foreflippers, and discard the rest of the turtle.

a circulatory system that transfers heat produced by the muscles back to the body core, enabling leatherbacks to maintain a body temperature up to 32°F (18°C) above the surrounding water temperature. Among other benefits, maintaining an elevated temperature enables leatherbacks to digest their food faster, boosting their growth rate.

Range

Leatherback turtles range over much of the world's oceans, with the exception of the Arctic and Antarctic regions. Their range extends from the Bering Sea, North Sea, Barents Sea, and Labrador Sea in the north to the waters bordering southern Chile and New Zealand in the South Pacific, and Argentina in the South Atlantic. There are small but significant genetic and physical differences between Atlantic and Pacific leatherbacks. Atlantic leatherbacks, for instance, grow considerably larger than those in the Pacific.

Development

Leatherback hatchlings are larger than those of any other sea turtle. Upon emerging from the nest, they scramble into the ocean and swim offshore for at least six days. After this brief period, they are not seen again for at least four years. Except for nesting females, leatherbacks remain completely pelagic for their entire lives. They do not reside in any single area, but make prodigious transoceanic voyages to exploit food resources that appear on a seasonal or temporary basis. Small juveniles likely remain in tropical waters, as their size does not permit them to store heat efficiently. Adults are uncommon in the tropics, except during the nesting season. The life span of leatherbacks is unknown, but a recent study suggests that they grow more than twice as fast as hard-shelled sea turtles, and mature early as well. The oldest age estimates in the small study sample were in the range of twenty to twenty-three years.

A leatherback turtle off the Azores Islands is surrounded by pilot fish. Because of their large size and pelagic habits, leatherbacks often function as mobile fish-aggregating devices. They are sometimes covered with remoras.

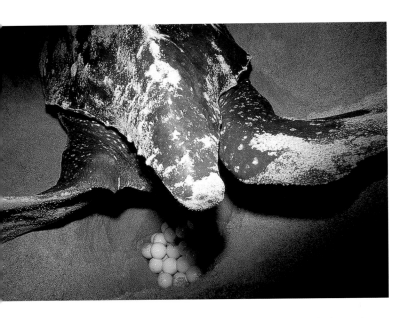

A leatherback lays her eggs on a beach in Trinidad. Leatherback eggs are valued as highly as those of any other sea turtle. This beach is now a protected area, but at the time the photo was taken, most nests, and many females, were poached. A gang of poachers armed with machetes surrounded the author as this picture was taken.

Diet

Even in the tropics, leatherbacks reach chilly waters by diving to depths of more than 3,900 feet (1,200 m). This places them in an elite class of air-breathing vertebrates, including sperm whales, bottlenose whales, and elephant seals, that are able to dive deeper than 3,300 feet (1,000 m). At these depths, leatherbacks reach a dense concentration of sea life known as the "deep-scattering layer." Located beneath clear tropical waters that are almost devoid of life, the deep-scattering layer is like a thick soup, with dense concentrations of sea jellies, gelatinous relatives of sea squirts, and other soft-bodied invertebrate prey.

Apart from an occasional scavenged fish or other floating item, these jelly-like organisms comprise almost the entire diet of leatherback turtles. This is remarkable because sea jellies consist of about 95 percent water; yet on this diet leatherbacks are able to grow both faster and larger than any other sea turtle. Apart from the water, the body of a sea jelly is mostly protein. To get enough energy to satisfy its metabolic needs, scientists have calculated that a leatherback would have to consume its own weight in sea jellies each day. To do this, leatherbacks must dive for food almost continuously around the clock without resting by night (or by day) like other sea turtles. At night the deep-scattering layer rises to shallower depths, so adult leatherbacks feed at night even more than by day (at least in the tropics). Small posthatchlings, however, are unable to dive deep and must confine their feeding to organisms that float close to the surface. Posthatchlings, therefore, feed mostly by day, when it is easier to see the prey. To hunt for prey, leatherbacks seek out boundaries between warmer and cooler water masses, areas where sea jellies (and fishing boats) tend to congregate.

Reproduction

A study of growth lines in tiny bones found in the eyes of leatherback turtles produced a preliminary estimate of about thirteen years for the average age at sexual maturity. After reaching maturity, female leatherbacks migrate between their feeding grounds, often in cool, high-latitude waters, and the tropical breeding beaches needed to incubate their eggs. Leatherbacks tend to nest on beaches that are open to the sea and steeper in slope than those preferred by other sea turtles, perhaps because on a steeper beach they do not have to drag their enormous bulk as far to get beyond the high-tide mark.

On average, females make the breeding migration every two to four years. Unlike other sea turtles, researchers do not know if many male leatherbacks also migrate to the breeding areas. Mating has been observed in the vicinity of the breeding beaches on only a couple of occasions. Females often nest almost immediately after arriving in the tropics, while their eggs presumably must be fertilized several weeks before nesting, so researchers have concluded that most mating must occur elsewhere.

Females usually lay four to seven clutches per season at intervals of nine to ten days. This is more clutches at shorter intervals than most other sea turtles. Leatherback eggs are the largest of any sea turtle—closer to the size of a racquetball than a ping-pong ball. However, the leatherback usually deposits a number of small yolkless eggs in each nest as well. Clutch size ranges from 46 to 160, with one-fifth to more than one-half of the eggs being tiny and yolkless. The smaller eggs are usually laid last, and may serve to prevent sand from filling in the spaces between the eggs and hampering gas exchange. The incubation time is fifty to seventy-eight days, depending upon the weather.

Leatherbacks tend to return to nest repeatedly in the same area, which is believed to be the nesting area where they hatched themselves. In the leatherback, however, this "nesting site fidelity" is not always as strong as in other sea turtles. In some areas they have more of a tendency to wander and try other nesting sites.

The breeding migrations of leatherbacks can be phenomenal. A leatherback feeding in Monterey Bay, California, was tracked to a breeding area in New Guinea, 6,000 miles (9,600 km) away. One that nested in South America crossed the Atlantic to West Africa. Eight leatherbacks nesting in Costa Rica all followed a narrow migration corridor, passing by the Galápagos Islands on their way into the South Pacific.

Conservation Status

By seeking out areas rich in marine life, where both fish and sea jellies congregate, leatherbacks expose themselves to the ever-increasing amounts of fishing gear concentrated in these locations. They are very susceptible to capture by drift nets and longlines. They rarely attempt to take the bait on a longline, but can easily become entangled or snag a flipper or other body part on a hook, possibly while investigating the chemical light-sticks that are frequently used as attractants on longlines. The light produced by these devices is similar to that produced by some of the jelly-like organisms on which leatherbacks feed. Scientists blamed drift nets and longlines used to capture swordfish off Chile for the crash of the leatherback population that nests on the Pacific coast of Mexico. In shallow waters off the nesting beaches, leatherbacks are susceptible to capture by trawl nets. This was one factor in the destruction of the large nesting population in Malaysia, although egg harvest was mostly to blame.

Because of their oily flesh, leatherbacks are only

Volunteers weigh a female leatherback at a nesting beach on the Pacific coast of Mexico. This one weighed 1,200 pounds (550 kg). Females attain even larger sizes in the Atlantic.

taken for food in a few parts of the world. But the combination of accidental drownings in fishing gear and egg harvesting has been devastating enough to lead some scientists to declare that leatherbacks are on the verge of extinction in the Pacific. The Atlantic population may be stable or even on the rise. Leatherbacks are listed as Endangered by both the United States and Australia and as Critically Endangered internationally by the IUCN.

CHAPTER 9

Watching Sea Turtles

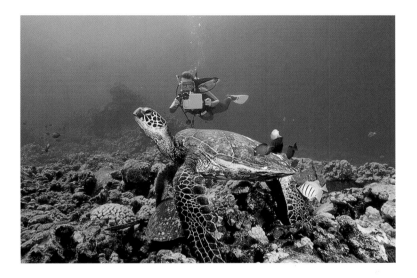

ABOVE: It is possible to videotape or photograph fascinating behavioral relationships, such as the symbiotic association between sea turtle and cleaner fish, if the diver moves slowly, keeps a respectful distance, and observes rather than disturbs.

LEFT: Diver and naturalist Norine Rouse observes a hawksbill turtle off Palm Beach, Florida. In areas where sea turtles are not hunted, divers who stay calm, breathe easy, and do not chase wildlife are often treated to close views of turtles.

ew activities in life are as enjoyable and as fascinating as observing wild animals in their natural environment. Watching wildlife is a great way to reconnect with the natural world while learning about the other species with which we share this planet. Watching sea turtles, both from land and from underwater, is no exception.

Because sea turtles emerge from the water at somewhat predictable times and places, they are among the easiest to observe of all sea creatures. It is important to keep in mind, however, that sea turtles usually come ashore only to lay eggs, and this is a particularly sensitive time for them. Observing wildlife carries with it the responsibility not to disturb the animal, especially when it is conducting vital activities, such as reproduction, feeding, or resting. Harassing sea turtles by grabbing or chasing them is cruel, irresponsible, and illegal under the Endangered Species Act.

Watching From Land

It is possible to observe sea turtles nesting throughout much of the tropics and subtropics—even in some major metropolitan areas. In most sea turtle nesting areas, visitors can join a guided tour to watch them. This is the ideal way to view nesting turtles, because it provides both the most satisfying experience for the viewer and the least chance of disturbing the turtle.

When on a turtle nesting beach, keep the following guidelines in mind. Use lights sparingly or not at all. Moving lights carry a particularly high risk of "spooking" a turtle before it nests. Loud sounds, especially sudden ones, may also spook a turtle, although at times turtles have been known to ignore them. It is best to leave dogs and other pets at home. When you see a turtle, crouch down and remain still until the turtle has made its nest and started to lay eggs. Only approach a nesting turtle from behind, and never

A trained naturalist (holding the light in this photo) shines a narrow-beam flashlight on only the nest cavity of this loggerhead turtle. Flashlights should only be turned on after the guide has indicated that it is okay to do so (usually after the turtle has commenced laying), and should be kept out of the turtle's eyes.

A shark's-eye view of a green turtle. Turtles will allow divers to swim close underneath only where they have been treated gently by humans in the past.

Oceanariums, such as this one at Atlantis Resort in the Bahamas, provide opportunities to view sea turtles. Their behavior when in captivity, however, differs markedly from their behavior in the wild.

touch the turtle. Flash photography is prohibited in many nesting areas. Where allowed, a flash should be used only after the turtle has commenced laying its eggs. If the turtle is tagged, record the number and inquire at the nearest university or government wildlife agency for the turtle research unit. Remember that beaches where adults nest are also beaches where hatchlings emerge, so step carefully! Beaches are also often places where insects swarm. Lightweight, long-sleeved clothing is usually the best protection. If repellent is necessary, use rub-on varieties instead of aerosol sprays, which may spread the chemicals over a wide area, affecting turtles and other organisms in the environment.

Watching From the Water

Scuba divers, snorkelers, kayakers, and boaters may have the opportunity to observe sea turtles in the ocean. To make the most of your experience and ensure the safety of the turtles, keep the following guidelines in mind.

Sea turtles sometimes exhibit curiosity toward the humans they encounter underwater and may move toward motionless divers. Sudden movements in the direction of a turtle, however, will likely cause it to flee. Any approach toward a turtle that is resting in one

This green turtle invites the cleaner fish to approach by perching high on its flippers with its neck outstretched. The turtle also adopts this pose when it is on the verge of fleeing. If a resting turtle rises up on its fins as a diver approaches, the diver should stop or back off.

After many years of legal protection, green sea turtles in Hawaii have become so habituated to humans that many will allow divers to approach them for a close look. In former years, sea turtles would flee if they saw a diver in the distance (in many areas where turtles are still hunted or harassed, sea turtles still behave this way). These fearless turtles, however, will be easy targets if turtle hunting is re-opened, as some Hawaiians are requesting.

spot should be made with caution while watching for signs of stress. A turtle that suddenly rises up on its pectoral fins, gapes with an open beak, or swipes its pectoral fin across its face is giving a signal that it is uncomfortable, and is probably about to flee. Treat any change in the turtle's behavior as a signal to stop and wait, or back off. Sea turtles are generally most cautious when breathing at the surface. Approaching one at this time either from underwater or at the surface may prompt the turtle to dive suddenly, without fully replenishing its air supply. Touching any wild animal, including sea turtles, is usually a very bad idea. People who observe sea turtles for extended periods without threatening them may find that the turtles eventually begin to interact with them or, even better, the turtles begin to ignore them and go about their daily turtle business. When this happens, observers are treated to a rare glimpse into the lives of these fascinating survivors from the Age of Dinosaurs.

Recommended Reading and Web Sites

Carr, Archie. *The Sea Turtle—So Excellent a Fishe.* Austin, TX: University of Texas Press, 1967, 1996.

Carr, Archie. *The Windward Road.* Gainesville, FL: University Press of Florida, 1955, 2000.

Davidson, Osha Gray. *Fire in the Turtle House: The Green Sea Turtle and the Fate of the Ocean.* New York: Public Affairs, 2001.

Orenstein, Ronald. *Survivors in Armor: Turtles, Tortoises & Terrapins.* Toronto, Canada: Key Porter Books, 2001.

Ripple, Jeff. *Sea Turtles.* Stillwater, MN: Voyageur Press, 1996.

For More Information Contact:

National Save The Sea Turtle Foundation
http://www.savetheseaturtle.org
4419 West Tradewinds Avenue
Ft. Lauderdale, Florida 33308
Tel: 954-351-9333
Toll Free: 1-877-TURTLE3

Caribbean Conservation Corporation
http://cccturtle.org/
4424 NW 13th Street, Suite #A1
Gainesville, FL 32609
Tel: 352-373-6441
Toll Free: 1-800-678-7853
Fax: 352-375-2449

Sea Turtle Restoration Project
http://www.seaturtles.org
P.O. Box 400, 40 Montezuma Avenue
Forest Knolls, CA 94933
Tel: 415-488-0370
Fax: 415-488-0372

Ocean Conservancy
http://www.oceanconservancy.org/
1725 DeSales Street, Suite 600
Washington, D.C. 20036
Tel: 202-429-5609

Sea Turtle Researchers' Site
http://www.seaturtle.org

Hawaiian Green Turtles
http://www.turtles.org

Mediterranean Turtles
http://www.euroturtle.org

NOAA Sea Turtle Pages
http://www.nmfs.noaa.gov/prot_res/
PR3/Turtles/turtles.html

Wider Caribbean Sea Turtle Network
http://www.widecast.org /

Australian Sea Turtles
http://www.ea.gov.au/coasts/
species/turtles/

Sea Turtle Navigation
http://www.unc.edu/depts/geomag/

U.S. government recovery plans for endangered species, including sea turtles
http://www.nmfs.noaa.gov/prot_res/
readingrm/Recoverplans/

Decline of the Sea Turtles (online book—National Academy Press, 1990)
http://bob.nap.edu/books/
030904247X/html/

Sea Turtle Symposium Proceedings
http://www.nmfs.noaa.gov/prot_res/
PR3/Turtles/symposia.html

Sea Turtles of the Californias
http://baja.seaturtle.org/
Southern California

WiLDCOAST
757 Emory St. PMB 161
Imperial Beach, CA 91932
Tel: 619-423-8530
Fax: 619-423-8488

Sea Turtles of Japan
http://www.umigame.org

Sea Turtles of India
http://www.kachhapa.org

Glossary

aquatic—living in the water

arribada—a mass nesting of sea turtles, roughly defined as more than 100 nests per day on a beach

benthic—bottom-dwelling

carapace—the black plate, or upper section, of a turtle's shell

carnivorous—meat-eating

CITES—Convention on International Trade in Endangered Species of Wild Flora and Fauna

cloaca—a common opening found in most vertebrates (including many fish and reptiles) and some invertebrates that provides an outlet for the digestive and reproductive tracts

clutch (of eggs)—all of the eggs laid in a single nest by one female

countershading—a color pattern that is dark on top and light underneath

crustacean—group of marine invertebrates—including crabs, lobsters, and shrimp—with jointed legs, segmented bodies, and shells made of chitin

cryptic—hidden or camouflaged, not obvious

dermal—relating to the skin

desiccation—the process of drying out

developmental migration—the period during which a posthatchling turtle grows into a juvenile while drifting and swimming across large areas of open ocean (a.k.a. "pelagic phase"). Developmental migration can also refer to travel from one developmental habitat to another as a turtle matures.

dinoflagellate—single-celled microorganisms that are propelled by flagella, or tiny whip-like extensions

diurnal—active by day

extirpation—elimination of a species in one part of its range

extinction—elimination of a species throughout its entire range

feral—refers to an animal of a domesticated breed that has "gone wild"

headstarting—the process of raising hatchling turtles in captivity to improve their survival through the vulnerable first few weeks to a year of life. Headstarting has not been proven to be effective and, in some cases, may even be counterproductive.

hatchling—in the strictest sense, "hatchling" refers to a turtle no more than three days old that is still living off of the egg yolk.

herbivorous—feeding on plant matter, vegetarian

invertebrate—animal without a backbone

lunar month—28 days

magnetite—the mineral form of black iron oxide, sometimes naturally magnetically polarized, which occurs in small amounts in a wide range of biological organisms.

mollusc (mollusk)—a member of a group of invertebrates with soft bodies that are usually protected by a shell. Octopus, squid, sea slugs, snails, clams, oysters, and most other sea shells are all examples of molluscs.

MtDNA (mitochondrial DNA)—DNA that occurs outside the nucleus and is passed intact in the egg from the mother to the offspring. MtDNA is not mixed with genes from the male parent like nuclear DNA.

natal—referring to the place of birth or, in the case of reptiles, birds, etc., where the animal hatched

natal homing—movement directly toward the hatching site or birthplace

nocturnal—active by night

omnivorous—feeding on both plant and animal matter

ovipositor—a tubular organ that extends from beneath the tail of a female turtle to deposit eggs into the nest

pelagic—dwelling in open ocean (usually surface waters), not linked to any point on the bottom

pheromone—a chemical that is used to communicate with another member of the same species or that produces a behavioral or physiological response in other members of the species

plastron—the belly plate or lower section of a turtle's shell that covers its underside

population—a breeding unit within a species. Members of a population normally breed together. A population is usually geographically isolated from other populations of the same species, but is not prevented by biological barriers from breeding with other populations. Usually one population will mix with others to a limited degree.

posthatchling—a small juvenile that has consumed its egg yolk and has begun to capture its own food

rookery—breeding area

scutes—horny plates, or scales, that cover the shells and skin of sea turtles

species—a biological unit of organisms that are capable of breeding together under normal circumstances and producing viable (fertile) offspring. (Please note that while hybrids between different sea turtle species are well-known, they are not common and their fertility has not been established.)

stimuli—signals perceived by the senses that provoke some sort of response (plural of stimulus)

TED (turtle excluder device, or "trawling efficiency device")—a trap door that dumps turtles out of shrimp nets and saves them from drowning

terrestrial—living on land

turbid—cloudy, dark, or stirred up; containing suspended sediment or other particles

vertebrate—animal with a backbone

Index